THE **EVIL**

AND

THE **INNOCENT**

SENATOR BILL DIAMOND

authorHOUSE®

AuthorHouse™
1663 Liberty Drive
Bloomington, IN 47403
www.authorhouse.com
Phone: 1-800-839-8640

Published by AuthorHouse 3/29/2012

ISBN: 978-1-4685-6497-6 (sc)
ISBN: 978-1-4685-6496-9 (hc)
ISBN:978-1-4685-6495-2 (e)

Library of Congress Control Number: 2012904887

THANK YOU

I STARTED WRITING this book in December 2010 and finally finished (before the serious editing started) on November 21, 2011. During those eleven months it was not unusual to be secluded in my home office with the door closed for hours at a time. I want to thank my family for understanding my commitment to do whatever it took to write this book. I know I was absent from your lives many times.

I was blessed to have extraordinary people help me in a variety of ways. Dr. Christian Potholm, Professor at Bowdoin College, who was always available at any time of day or night to advise me and answer my continuously annoying questions. I appreciate his loyalty and support.

I couldn't have written this book without the courageous people who were willing to share their personal stories. Bringing back the memories of the pain and suffering they experienced as victims was very difficult for them. And yet, they did so without hesitation because they realized that by sharing their own horrific stories they will make a difference in the lives of children who are being sexually assaulted and abused today. I also appreciate the individuals who were willing to tell their stories as sexual predators and users of online child pornography. They were willing to step up and take responsibility for their actions.

To Lieutenant Glenn Lang and his team at the Maine Computer Crimes Unit who provided invaluable information for this book, I extend my deepest appreciation. They literally rescue sexually abused children and arrest sexual predators -- what more needs to be said.

I extend my special thanks to Carol Kontos who spent an inordinate amount of time and energy editing every page of this book. Her expertise and knowledge provided the necessary ingredient needed to make my manuscript presentable to the publisher.

To all the people who will go unnamed yet provided moral support and valuable commentary as the book was being created, I say thank you.

DEDICATION

I DEDICATE THIS book to my mother, Elsie Fellows Emery. She taught me how to survive and to be ready to help others as the first thought of every day. She was courageous without knowing it was a virtue, and forever giving to others without knowing she was unique. She passed away February 26, 2012, at the age of 87-years-old and left a legacy I could never hope to match.

I also dedicate this book to my maternal grandfather, Ralph Fellows, who was a small, two-horse, dirt farmer in West Gardiner, Maine. He never had much, only his dreams of a better life for his family. He was my father figure during the developmental years of my life and taught me well. When riding the old farm horse either in the hayfield hauling hay or in the woods cutting pulp, he would always say, "if you get scared or lost or unsure of yourself, just stay on the horse and it will get you back to the barn." At various times in my life I have been be scared or would lose my focus and wouldn't know where to turn or just wanted to give up. Whenever that happened I always remembered what he told me. I stayed on the horse and it has always got me back to the barn.

This book is also dedicated to all of the children who have survived sexual assaults and … for those who didn't. I will not give up.

TABLE OF CONTENTS

PREFACE

"MY BACKGROUND MADE ME DO IT"

As a Maine State Senator for the past seven years, I have researched, written, cosponsored, and sponsored over 50 proposed laws and amendments pertaining to sex offenders and the sex offender registry for consideration by the Maine Legislature. Many of these documents have, in fact, become laws in the State of Maine. They were all designed to improve Maine's Sex Offender Registry, to protect children from sexual predators, and to provide needed funding and organizational support for the Maine State Police Computer Crimes Unit. From 2004 – 2008 I was the Senate Chairman of the Joint Standing Committee on Criminal Justice and Public Safety of the Maine Legislature and in that capacity conducted hundreds of public hearings and managed a similar number of committee work sessions relating to sexual predators and the system that prosecutes, incarcerates, and monitors their whereabouts. My efforts were focused on studying every aspect of the problems associated with sex offenders and the sex offender registry, which was originally created to protect the citizens and to be a useful tool for law enforcement agencies. I have also spent many years studying and becoming familiar with the behind-the- scenes operations of the Maine Computer Crimes Unit. This unit is comprised of law enforcement professionals whose primary purpose is rescuing children who are subjects of sexual abuse and to identify, locate, and arrest the sexual predators who prey on these children. Having the rare opportunity to witness and observe the little known strategies and investigative techniques conducted by the Computer Crimes Unit has given me an exceptional insight into their internal operations. This research has provided me with valuable and unique information that I enthusiastically share with the readers of this book.

I also served eight years as *Maine's Secretary of State* which included overseeing the Bureau of Motor Vehicles, a responsibility that required a close association with the Maine State Police, the Office of the Attorney General, and county and local law enforcement agencies. As Secretary of State, and later as a state Senator, I had the opportunity to work with the various Commissioners of the Department of Public Safety and heads of the Maine State Police studying their organizational structure and the critical issues pertaining to public safety.

During the years as Senate Chair of the Criminal Justice and Public Safety (CJ&PS) Committee the infamous and internationally reported, *2006 "Maine Easter Murders"* were committed by an assailant who used Maine's Sex Offender Registry as a resource to locate and kill his victims. This vigilante-style attack resulted in an in-depth legislative study, by the Criminal Justice and Public Safety Committee, which examined the structure and purpose of Maine's Sex Offender Registry. This extensive review resulted in a greater understanding of the problems and consequences associated with the registry.

I have worked with six Maine Governors -- James Longley, Joseph Brennan, John "Jock" McKernan, Angus King, John Baldacci and Paul LePage, and their respective administrations relating to the issues contained in this book. I also appreciate the opportunity to have worked with district attorneys, trial lawyers, advocacy groups, members of the Judiciary, law enforcement agencies, and national organizations identifying weaknesses and strengths in the sex offender registries and pinpointing flaws in our current sex offender statutes.

Prior to my service in state government, I spent over 20 years as a professional educator as a teacher, principal and superintendent of schools. I started teaching 5th grade in 1968 and during the next two decades had the wonderful opportunity to teach grades 6, 8, 10, and 12, and held the various aforementioned administrative positions. Working in those capacities enhanced my interests and concerns relating to the constant vulnerability of children. Now more than ever, mostly due to the Internet, children are more vulnerable to predators and thus, in more danger of sexual assault in some manner. The teaching profession, including administrators and school boards, can and should play a key role in creating an awareness program for students, teachers and parents on how to protect children in this new age of technology. Hopefully this book will assist in accomplishing that goal. Prevention - through education and awareness – is an essential piece of the puzzle. In many ways, it may be the most important.

Having been blessed with a teaching/administrative background has given me unique insights regarding the needs of children that became the foundation on which this book was built. It's been an intense relationship with a subject that tears my heart out, but I couldn't stop telling the story even when the horrific details of abuse kept leaping out at me from the hundreds of pages of research – leaving me with a bruised mind and a blistered soul.

INTRODUCTION

THE POTENTIAL interest in this book could be measured by the following fact – for the past 3 years the online website for the Maine Sex Offender Registry has had <u>8 million</u> hits a year!

The *Evil and the Innocent* presents a <u>*real life and true*</u> inside look at the tragedies and suffering of the victims of sexual assault. Those who committed these crimes against the innocent will be described and discussed in detail revealing the sadistic fantasies that swirl in the heads of these child sex offenders and how these fantasies manifest themselves into reality with total disregard for the pain and suffering inflicted on the victims – children and infants. These are <u>*real and actual*</u> cases that expose heartbreaking and sometimes nauseating facts of sexual assaults and molestations. As difficult as it may be for the reader, these documented details are openly displayed in the book and will stay with the reader for a long time. The devastating images that imprint on the walls of your mind like scary nightmare faces will flash back to you without warning. These "reruns" have no schedule, only the startling reality of appearing randomly when you least expect them. I have been dealing with these images for years after seeing the dead eyes and helpless faces of little children who suffered the onslaught of cruel and inhumane acts by the evilness of those who, in their desire to achieve personal sexual gratification, tore out the very souls of their innocent victims.

This book may startle and sicken you because of the cold, hard, facts that until now have been mostly hidden from you. Why? To protect you. It is my strong belief that the real life suffering must be brought into the light of day so the collective "you" demands that it stop – no matter the cost.

The complexities of creating effective and fair laws to protect the innocent and punish the evil and still meet constitutional standards are thoroughly examined – and the goal of enacting successful legislation will be achieved.

The cases of sexual assault and abuse described in this book are all true and you may find the details very disturbing and gut wrenching – I hope so. Even though many of these real life experiences and descriptions are about attacks that happened in Maine, there are also references to nationally known sexual assault cases with similar descriptions provided with the same gruesome details. Unfortunately, violent sex offenses happen all too frequently in every state in this country and around the world. The situations you will read about in these chapters will be horrifying and cause you to question the very humanity of some people, or the lack thereof, in this world. You will ask, "WHY?"

The Evil and the Innocent focuses on the complete cast of characters who, for various reasons, become engulfed in the all-consuming tragedy of sexual abuse. Those who prey on the most vulnerable - children and infants - inflicting pain, life long psychological scars and even death -- they are the *evil*. The victims, who are used for sexual gratification and twisted pleasures by those who treat them as nothing more than helpless prey – they are the *Innocent*. There are also those who have been categorized as evil simply because of their required placement on a sex offender registry. Some of these individuals are not totally innocent, but they certainly do not pose a risk to anyone so they shouldn't be placed in the mix with violent sexual predators and create unnecessary anxiety among the public.

The tragic murders, sexual assaults and ongoing abuse of children that I have chronicled occurred and often continued for several, preventable reasons, most commonly because people didn't pay attention to signals sent by the victims. Signals include how they play, how they interact with other children and even how they dress. Another reason is that the perpetrator had such a good disguise so was never considered to be a danger to anyone, the least of all, to children.

You will also read about some of the nationally known cases involving young children who were kidnapped and used for deviant sexual pleasures before being murdered. Specifically, these are cases where children were raped, sodomized, tortured and dismembered for the specific purposes of satisfying the sexual pleasures of those who "get off" looking at videos and other images depicting these real life abuses. Those who purchase, watch and share these images play a significant role in feeding the never-ending demand for "fresh faces and new bodies" for the prolific child pornography industry.

Efforts to find and save these children are usually unsuccessful because of the extensive and sophisticated network of the Internet child porn cult, which is designed to protect its members and supporters with carefully concealed identities incorporating in-depth and painstaking screening methods of would-be customers. After being used and their "value diminished" because of injury, illness or just becoming the "same old, same old" to the viewers, the infants and children are considered to be damaged goods. This is only a problem until there is a suitable replacement - then the child simply then becomes a *"throw-away"* by the industry.

Maybe a child even becomes a candidate for a live-filmed killing known as a "snuff". Because of these reasons there is a constant need for more children, more infants – more victims. To satisfy the demand for more "little sex stars," children are kidnapped, utilized from within a family or are taken advantage of by unsuspecting neighbors and friends. There are many fetishes and fantasies to satisfy resulting in a constant need for babies and children of all ages. The child porn industry will pay a high price to keep their paying customers happy – and so will the children.

You will read about courage and determination and how kids learned to survive even under the most terrible of conditions. The details contained in these pages of sexual assaults against infants will be devastating and very difficult to read, but it is important that the public, elected officials, and the media no longer sanitize these tragic and all too common cases of severe child abuse. As disgusting and hurtful as it may be for you to learn about the specifics of how and why a 24-month old baby is filmed while being sexually assaulted by a full grown man by penetrating his erect penis into the baby's vagina - these facts need to be told so *there will be outrage.* If not, nothing will change.

It is understandable that we as a society try to protect ourselves from knowing the horrible realities of these abuses. However, until we are able to make the public understand the sexual assaults on our children that are happening in our churches, schools, homes, and neighborhoods these abuses will not be eliminated or even reduced. These assaults will, in fact, continue as they currently do, going unnoticed just below the surface of our daily routines. They are like cancer cells running through our veins unseen until, without warning, there they are - striking fear in our hearts. We need to see what's happening – what's really happening - in our own communities and there needs to be an awareness of the reality of the ongoing sexual abuse of our children. The public needs to see details, specifics and real faces on real children. What are we waiting for? If these chapters inspire the readers to demand change then the purpose of researching and writing this book has been fulfilled. Of course, I'm hoping for thousands of new advocates who are disgusted, enraged, and demanding change after seeing what is revealed.

Raising the level of outrage and intolerance towards those who sexually attack children will provide the motivation for our political leaders around the country to support the necessary funding to effectively battle and significantly reduce sexual abuse. Making this battle a top priority - at least as important as protecting vernal pools, killing coyotes and deciding the state dessert - is key to making the important changes in our sex offender laws. It can be argued that if we as a society place the same importance on protecting our children from sexual assault as we do on other special interest issues, like campaigning to pass a special interest referendum, then there would be a significant impact on improving our policies and procedures dealing with child abuse.

In Maine, as in most states, getting the necessary resources to fight this problem is difficult, to say the least. The high level technology used to identify, track and capture predators and to rescue victims is costly and highly trained professionals are required to maximize the resources. Fighting this battle costs money – significant amounts of money. In relation to other state funded programs it must rise to the top when competing for available funding. It's time to raise holy hell about this problem and say, "Enough is Enough!" We can make a difference if we put our minds to it and if we make our legislators part of the solution, but they have to hear a unified and loud voice from all of us. Nothing else will work to protect our children and grandchildren.

The plan outlined in this book details how we should move forward to provide our law enforcement agencies with the tools necessary to rescue captured children and outlines critical steps needed to prevent violent sexual predators from gaining access to their prey. The plan provides a framework for a better and more efficient sex offender registry that establishes a reliable and understandable source of information for the interested public and law enforcement agencies. You will see that designing the best possible system to accomplish the goals needed to protect our children is relatively inexpensive – even though the costs are significantly more compared to what is currently spent now. To have waited this long to make these bold, albeit common sense, changes in our public safety procedures is frustrating given the importance that is always placed on protecting our kids – at least that's what they all say.

It is the hope that this book will energize and motivate you, the caring public, to insist that those in influential positions in government hear your demands for change. The intent is to encourage people in key positions to exercise leadership to implement the steps outlined in these pages and to appropriately address ways to effectively manage sex offenders and to initiate the obvious changes that should be made to our current laws. This is essential to fix a broken system – a system more broken now than ever.

PROLOGUE

I'LL TELL WHO I WANT

"I WAS STANDING by my bicycle in the corner of a large parking lot not far from my home when he drove up and got out of his big car and told me that my mother said that it was alright to go with him to buy some flowers for his wife – then he put my bicycle next to a tree, grabbed me by my arm and put me in his car. We drove off to a hidden place where he made me perform oral sex on him and do other things. I was crying and scared and wanted to go home. After he finished I felt his hands on my neck."

She was only ten years old on that day in May 1989 around 5 in the afternoon, but the violence she experienced over the next several hours, until he finally left her for dead, was something no one could imagine would happen in a small town in Maine. It was especially shocking since this predator was someone who lived in the same apartment building in Saco, Maine as the girl and her family. He was a man she knew very well. She delivered his daily newspaper to him and would go to his apartment on a regular basis to collect money for her deliveries. But on that afternoon, Joseph J. Tellier, the man she thought she knew so well, sexually assaulted, strangled and left her, a helpless little girl, for dead.

"He told me that he would take me home, but first he said we were going to have a little fun." He then told her to take her clothes off and she remembers crying and asking him to please take her to her friend's house, which she had remembered passing on Route 5 as he drove to the secluded, wooded area at the end of a narrow dirt road in Limerick, Maine.

"After he had finished doing things to me and making me do things to him – which was a long time lasting for four or five hours - I remember him telling me not to tell anyone about what had happened – that this was just between the two of us, but I said that I would tell who I want. That was probably a big mistake."

Uttering those few words of defiance could have very well been the reason that he decided to make sure that she *didn't* tell anyone. The next thing she remembers was Tellier putting his big hands on her shoulders. She was putting her clothes back on as she sat back to him in the front seat of his old grey Oldsmobile, the kind with the big bench seats, which to a little girl seemed like the size of a small bed. "He started choking me and that is the last thing I remembered until I regained my consciousness several hours later between 5-5:30 the next morning."

She remembers opening her eyes and being covered with dirt and leaves. Her first thought was instant fear; frightened beyond imagination that her attacker might still be near. To her relief, he was nowhere around having left her for dead in a shallow grave carefully hidden from sight. The "grave" was a natural depression in the ground that was large enough for a child and did not require much digging. By the position of her body when she regained consciousness, it appeared that he had rolled her into the sunken, hollowed out area with her body ending up lying on the right side. The right cheek of her face was pressed on the ground with the left arm positioned over her head.

Because there were burns on her upper left arm, which was the part of her body closest to the surface, it was believed that Tellier had attempted to drive his vehicle over the "grave" for the purpose of packing down the surface. In doing so, the vehicle's hot muffler had probably come in contact with the little girl's skin through the thin layers of dirt and leaves.

After managing to crawl out, cold and shivering and covered with dirt and debris, she noticed that the right side of her face was bloody, "It was like someone had put acid on my face and my skin was just hanging in small pieces and feeling very raw."

She started looking around to determine the best way to escape that horrible place and immediately realized that what she saw just ahead was a somewhat familiar narrow dirt road, with the thick, mangled brush that seemed to be reaching up from the ditches ready to grab whomever walked by. This unusually observant little girl remembered that when Tellier was driving them into the woods she had noticed a tree with a baby's diaper dangling from its limb. While trying to find the best way out, Michelle noticed again that same diaper hanging in the tree, reaching out like a helpful hand with reassurance that she was heading in the right direction. Somehow, that diaper gave her a small but comforting sense that everything was going to be okay.

As Michelle continued on the journey, she walked over a small, narrow, wooden, bridge where once again a helpful flashback came to mind as she remembered seeing two people fishing as Tellier's car drove over that bridge on the way to the secluded hide-a-way. She remembers pressing her face against the window of the car and trying desperately to make eye contact with both people, hoping that they would see the fear in the eyes and hear the silent screams from a captured child who needed help. The messages from her eyes were to no avail, as the slow moving and deliberate, hearse-like vehicle had moved toward its destination.

Later, as her confusion cleared, her head the brave girl found herself walking on the side of Route 5 with cars and trucks speeding by on their early morning commute. No one even slowed down to check on what should have been at least a curious sight – a little girl in somewhat of a daze - walking with no shoes, the right side of her face bloody, looking very out of place, her clothes covered with dirt and obviously in need of help. "I remember thinking, 'Why isn't anyone stopping?' because I was like - a little kid walking on a major highway at 6 o'clock in the morning not looking normal." That "little kid" showed determination - well beyond her 10 years – during that 12-hour nightmare. Today that same determination partly describes Michelle Tardif, a 32 year-old mother of two children who never lost that courage and focus.

Eventually that morning little Michelle randomly stopped at what she remembers as being "a little red house" and asked for help. The police were notified and the girl that had been through so much was quickly taken to the hospital for medical treatment. After the long ordeal that would forever change Michelle's life, the molested and bloody survivor was finally rescued.

"I remember coming in (to the hospital) on a stretcher and my parents being on each side of me," Michelle recalled. Immediately upon arriving at the hospital, she received the critically important physical examination that is required to gather evidence of rape and sexual assault followed by the necessary medical attention. Sometimes it seems like this standard operating procedure is backwards in that the first priority should be the need to attend to any medical needs first then performing the examination to secure evidence. However, in theses types of cases the accepted policy is, considering the medical condition of the patient is determined to be stable, to secure the potential evidence from the patient, thus giving the police the best possible chance of identifying the attacker.

The right side of her face was still bloody with pieces of skin still hanging like drops of white paste from her cheek, lower jaw and part of her forehead. She had received many bruises and lacerations over her body and face from the attack. The trauma of forced sexual assault on her body and mind was bad enough. Having to go through the additional humiliation of examinations, part of which Michelle remembered as, "those awful stirrups," was a difficult memory. For anyone, especially a young girl, to have to be subjected to this invasive probing process of gathering physical evidence such as semen, pubic hairs, and blood, is frightening for sure. Then having to endure the embarrassing questions concerning descriptions and details about the attacker, including any distinguishing characteristics of the genital area and other parts of the body, makes the entire process an excruciating experience.

The police acted quickly once they were informed about Michelle's abduction and based on the available information and evidence the suspect, Joseph J. Tellier or "Jay" as his neighbors called him, was immediately arrested. The police impounded Tellier's large, grey Oldsmobile that contained Michelle's blood and one of her shoes. The police also found Michelle's blood on Tellier's clothes and even secured the sheets from his bed looking for more physical evidence.

Following the attack and prior to the police arriving at Tellier's home the next morning to make the arrest, Michelle's mom was desperately searching for her missing daughter and at one point saw Tellier sitting on his porch. She asked him if he had seen Michelle. He said that he hadn't. The fact that he was so cavalier was understandable to Michelle who said, "He thought I was dead. There was no reason for him to worry about it." Little did he know that this young girl would literally "resurface.".

Tellier was charged with attempted murder, kidnapping and gross sexual assault. The prosecutors reduced the attempted murder charge as part of a plea bargain that ultimately resulted in a 24-year prison sentence.

Michelle's parents chose to proceed with this plea bargain to protect their child from the rigors of a trial. As a result, Tellier got off with a much lesser sentence than was deserved. To top it off, he actually served only about 15 years of the 24-year sentence due to "good behavior". (f1)

After Tellier was released from prison in 2004, he moved to Hollis, Maine. At that time, Michelle was 25 years old and lived with her young daughter in Saco – literally the next town over. When Michelle learned of his release, she was extremely concerned. Not only was this violent predator free after committing such a horrible crime, but he also would be living uncomfortably close to Michelle and her family. Salt in the wound – stick in the eye – arrogant defiance, all applied to Tellier's decision to live so closely to the person who was brutally used, not so long ago - as a "fun" object. Now having a young daughter of her own, Michelle was very worried that he would be on the streets *once again* moving about undetected and appearing without warning.

As frightening as the situation was for Michelle, there would be even more distressing news – unbelievable news. When inquiring about Maine's laws pertaining to mandatory registration of convicted sex offenders who are released from prison, Michelle discovered that Tellier would not have to register as a sex offender. He wouldn't have to provide any information about where he lived, worked or even the nature of the crimes committed to the public or to law enforcement. To Michelle and many others, such a lack of common sense in the law was absurd. A violent sexual predator like Tellier who committed such a terrible crime would *not* be required to register on the state *sex offender registry*, simply because the crime was committed a few years before the cut off date when sex offender registration was required. As far as Michelle was concerned, the law needed changing so she called upon the same courage and focus demonstrated twenty- two years earlier to accomplish her goal. This former "victim" instinctively employed the same determination and boldly confronted the legislature and the entire legal system in an effort to make sure the law was changed - and it was.

CHAPTER I

MICHELLE TARDIF'S living nightmare mandated that something be done. After all, how could the state allow people as dangerous as Joseph Tellier to live undetected in our communities without some formal notification to the public and to law enforcement agencies about their whereabouts? Michelle was correct. Leaving Tellier off the sex offender registry flew in the face of common sense and she made that point quite well when presenting testimony before the Legislature's Criminal Justice and Public Safety Committee on April 11, 2005. Part of her testimony was as follows:

> *Now answer this question, what makes him (Tellier) or any other person that committed these crimes prior to this date any better then the ones after? He's not. The term 'sexually violent predator' means a person who has been convicted of a sexually violent offense and who suffers from a mental abnormality or personal disorder that makes the person likely to engage in predatory sexually violent offenses. That was my attacker, that is all of them, not just the ones that committed crimes <u>after</u> June 30, 1992.*

Little did the committee know, that would be the day that Michelle Tardif's fortitude and determination would literally, by itself, set in motion the most significant changes in and legal challenges to the sex offender laws and the sex offender registry in Maine.

Members on the committee soon learned with a jolt of realism – the

1

rest of the story. Maybe State Representative Stan Gerzofsky, a veteran member of the Committee, said it best. "We closed one big loophole and opened a hundred more, not to mention pissing off the Maine Supreme Court." The loophole that allowed violent sex offenders like Tellier to avoid being placed on the sex offender registry was slammed shut, but in the process of doing so other doors were opened creating more significant problems that would continue to haunt the committee members, the legislature, and several other groups and individuals for years to come.

As the Senate Chairman of the committee in 2005, I can say without a doubt that each of us on the committee believed that changing the law by extending the time period when convicted sex offenders would be required to register from 1992 back to 1982 was certainly the right thing to do. Michelle Tardif was a walking, living example of what was wrong with the old law and it was clear to everyone what specifically needed to be changed. It was only common sense – right? After all, who could logically argue that violent predators like Joseph Tellier shouldn't have to register just because of an arbitrary date? Who could disagree that such a change was not only necessary, but should happen as soon as possible?

Notwithstanding our noble intentions, several unintended consequences were created from our change in the law that we didn't anticipate including the disruption of the lives of literally hundreds of people's lives who were convicted of sex related offenses (some of them low-level offenses) up to 23 years earlier, some being low level offenses, would now be placed on the sex offender registry for everyone to see. Sex offenders like Tellier were added to the registry and that was the intent and certainly was an improvement to the old law. The new law also, without discrimination, yanked people from their rightfully deserved private lives, people who were absolutely no threat to society in any way, and thrust them onto the public stage where they were ostracized and ridiculed, not to mention losing jobs and breaking up families. It's this latter group that the committee and legislature failed miserably. Scores of them decided to challenge the law in court saying this new requirement to register as a sex offender was an added penalty to an old conviction and was therefore unconstitutional – and they might have been right.

In the years prior to the existence of Maine's law requiring convicted sex offenders to register, several divorce cases were settled with one parent, usually the husband, agreeing to having committed to what might have seemed at the time to be a minor charge – inappropriate sexual touching or some other similar offense against a son or daughter. Often times these charges were made as each side tried to gain advantage over the other, especially in the more bitter divorces cases where such accusations were used for retaliation purposes. The commonly used strategy was to establish as many charges against the other as possible in an effort to build a maximum advantage in the negotiation process.

For example, a wife might accuse the husband of touching the daughter in a sexual manner in an attempt by the wife to either gain 100% custody of the child or simply as a way to punish, embarrass or gain the upper hand against the husband. The committee heard testimony specifically detailing such scenarios. For example, the husband was told that being convicted of the sexual offense would have no consequence (true at the time) relating to the divorce, and by pleading guilty to the charge he would then be allowed to see his children on a regular basis. Since it seemed like a minor issue at the time, accepting the terms of the agreement was an easy tradeoff.

Most sexual assault convictions that occurred during the new 10-year "look back" period would require immediate placement on the sex offender registry (SOR). Had that been known the accused would probably not have agreed to certain pleas resulting in placement on the registry. So, with the example of the divorce case, the husband, who agreed to a sex offense charge simply to get the divorce settled, was shocked to get a notice from the Maine State Police, 20 years after the divorce, informing the shocked recipient of the notice that he would now have to register with the state as a sex offender – immediately.

One such divorced father explained that he pleaded with his former wife for years literally begging her to recant what both knew was a fraudulent charge at the time of the divorce - sexual touching of the then teenage daughter. The former wife didn't dare to confess about lying and the now adult daughter refused to admit publicly that her father wasn't guilty for fear of embarrassing the mother – and so the snowball kept getting bigger and bigger. Therefore, when the new law was passed, his divorce settlement made in the mid 1980's was revisited, and out of the blue the former husband and father who was quietly living a happy life was now required to be placed on the sex offender registry. When his employer found out about this new sex offender status the bewildered man was fired from his long held job at Hannafords Foods. He was shunned by his neighbors and he experienced added stress from other concerned members of his family including his current wife.

Over the next few years, several people, who had been convicted of a variety of other sexual assault crimes testified before the committee, emphatically stating that they would never have agreed to what was believed at the time to be minor sexual assault charges had they realized that many years later there would be a new law requiring their names, addresses and "offense," to be publicized on the Internet. Placement on the sex offender registry can be devastating to the person having to register and, in some cases, even more so to the registrant's family members. As you will read later in this book, sometimes appearing on the sex offender registry can be fatal.

Furthermore, since many sex offender registries, including Maine's, do not make a discernable distinction between whether the registrant poses a high or low level of risk to the public, people naturally assume that everyone on the list is extremely dangerous, thus causing unnecessary fear and anxiety within the community. Most all agree that appearing on the registry is a life changing experience, deserved by some and unfair to others. However, even with that element of unfairness, one can argue that a sex offender registry does serve an important role both in protecting society from those who present potential risks to reoffend. There does need to be a balance between informing citizens about potentially dangerous sex offenders and needlessly ruining the lives of "low-risk" sex offenders as illustrated by testimonies of isolation, family breakups and fear of attack. These stories have been routinely told by those who, until the law was changed, were living private, normal lives.

So, the first unintended consequence of adding the extra 10-year "look back" to the law resulted in unnecessarily placing "low" or even "no-risk" sex offenders on the registry, which totally disrupted and, in some instances, devastated their lives.

Enter the Maine Supreme Judicial Court with their unanimous

opinion in the case, JOHN DOE v. DISTRICT ATTORNEY issued May 23, 2007. This appeal to the high court by a person simply known as John Doe, in an effort to conceal personal identity, was very significant because it would set the standard for many other convicted sex offenders waiting to see the full impact regarding required registration under the new law. The following are some of the more telling conclusions from that Court opinion.

This was a case based on a complaint alleging the following:

> *"…Doe, a Maine resident, was convicted and sentenced after 1982 and before 1986 for a sex offense he committed when he was nineteen years old on a family member, and to which he pleaded guilty. He was sentenced to less than seventy days of incarceration. He had previously been convicted of public indecency when he was eighteen years old. Doe's amended complaint states that since the sex offense conviction, he has not abused drugs or alcohol.*
>
> *He is gainfully employed and has worked almost continuously for almost twenty years. He married his current wife in 1988, and she has three children from a previous marriage. His wife told him that she will have to leave him if his name goes on the sex offender registry. He also states that he has reason to believe that he will lose his job if his name is placed on the registry and his neighbors will attempt to get him to leave the neighborhood. He is in fear of violence to his person."*

The complaint further states in part, "…*the retroactive provisions of SORNA (Maine's Sex Offender Registration and Notification Act) ….render the statute unconstitutional pursuant to the United States and Maine Constitutions. Doe alleges violations of …..due process because he was not informed of the registration requirements when he entered his guilty plea;*"

There is an important reference in the Maine and United States Constitution known as the, *Ex Post Facto Clause*, which reads, "…protects liberty by preventing governments from enacting statutes with 'manifestly unjust and oppressive' retroactive effects." The Maine Supreme Judicial

Court felt strongly that "…the Clause prohibits the application of a criminal statute to a defendant that makes more burdensome the punishment for a crime after its commission." (f5) The high court didn't say that being required to be placed on the sex offender registry was punishment, but did remand the case for trial to determine if the Sex Offender Registration and Notification Act is punitive or in violation of the ex post facto clause.

In other words, a person who was convicted of an offense and penalized accordingly could not be given an additional punishment at a later date because of a new law pertaining to that same offense that was not in existence at the time of the offense. Even though the courts have not found being on the registry as "punishment" most people who are familiar with the process acknowledge that it certainly causes serious problems as illustrated earlier. The issues before the courts pertained to fairness and further punishment regarding the requirements to re-register at various intervals *in- person* and the frequency of required re-registrations.

Not only did the Supreme Judicial Court articulate its serious concerns about the new law, but some justices went one step further. Justices, Donald Alexander and Warren Silver, issued a "Concurrence" to the Court's opinion.

They went on to say in part, "*…the subsequent retroactive application of SORNA (Sex Offender Registration and Notification Act) and imposition of internet registries, we have learned much about the stigmatizing effect of registration and notification. We now recognize the extent to which the State's use of the internet to display registration information correlates to the shaming and branding punishments used in colonial times, and we have seen the registries' potential for causing retributive and vigilante violence against registrants. Instead of locking the criminal in stocks in the town square or branding the offender with a letter to make the community aware of his crime, SORNA directs the State to place the registrant's personal information on the World Wide Web, labeled as an offender convicted of a heinous crime. Although calling the internet a 'modern day town square' may sound simplistic, much of our society's day-to-day communication occurs via the web, instead of in the markets and on the street corners. The ease with which any individual in the world can access a registry website and the accumulated personal data on the offenders makes the geographic reach of this information boundless.*

In our internet age, the 'shaming and branding' of sex offenders inevitably leads to community stigmatization and ostracism. Being branded a sex offender in a community indisputably has ostracizing effects, including social isolation, difficulty finding employment, and being targeted for harassment, violence, and even murder." (f5)

So the second shoe was dropped regarding the new "10-year look back" law. The Maine Supreme Judicial Court remanded the case for further fact finding to determine if it was constitutional. The justices indicated that the ex post facto issue could be a problem with this case. The mere act of requiring those convicted of a sex offense to be placed on the world-wide-web was another serious concern that could not be ignored.

To summarize, the Maine Supreme Judicial Court raised concerns about the requirements of the Sex Offender Registration and Notification Act, which included the sex offender registry, saying these requirements may violate the constitution and therefore remand (send back for consideration) to the court.

Dragging citizens from their well established private lives, people who literally posed no threat to anyone, and placing them on the sex offender registry was the harsh reality of the new law.

On the other hand, there were dangerous sex offenders who were convicted during that new 10-year look-back period who for the first time had to register – and that was a good result of the law.

The trick was to find a way to get at the evil in an effort to protect the innocent without hurting the bystanders. This became a significant challenge for the Maine Legislature and for most other legislatures around the country, resulting in litigation that is still unresolved and continues to increase in numbers.

The Maine Legislature took direction from the Supreme Judicial Court and passed important amendments to the law. (See Public Law, 2009, chapter 570). One change specified that a person sentenced on or after January 1, 1982 and prior to June 30, 1992 may be relieved of the duty to register if that person submits to the Department of Public Safety such a request to be excluded, and the person meets certain statutory requirements to qualify for removal, including, but not limited to:

1. The person was fully discharged from the correctional system prior to September 1, 1998.
2. The person's convictions did not include more than one Class A sex offense or equal to that offense from another jurisdiction (state).
3. The person had not been previously sentenced for a prior sex offense.

As of September 1, 2011 there have been 624 registrants previously on the sex offender registry who have been granted permission to be removed because of the above referenced law change. Of course, with this change comes the double-edged sword: with the newly acquired status of being unnoticed and undetected comes the ability to seek out victims more easily, if so desired.

Other changes to the law designed to satisfy the constitutionality and fairness questions were made. The courts were given more flexibility in sentencing, thus allowing a deviation from the previous strict guidelines that required sentencing to follow the Sex Offender Registration and Notification Act. In other words, in some cases more attention could be given to the individual cases when registration was involved. As of September 1, 2011, 2934 sex offenders remained on the Maine Sex Offender Registry. (f3)

In hindsight, it became obvious that the new law, that was a result of the valid concerns and the need to close the "Tellier loophole," became exhibit number one illustrating how lawmakers can take a well-intended idea and create a law that is good, bad and ugly. The law had some good results by requiring more dangerous sex offenders to register for the first time. It was bad for those citizens who, as a result of previous plea-bargaining, found themselves part of one of the most despised groups in our society. It was ugly in that the law, by its very nature, continues to be a catalyst for new amendments to be filed in a piece-meal fashion, thus missing the necessary global visionary attention required in formulating this type of legislation. Legislators have the knowledge and skill to create comprehensive, bold and effective laws structured to ensure safety for our citizens and still maintain fairness while avoiding constitutional objections – but will they?

On August 18, 2011, Kennebec County Superior Court Justice Michaela Murphy rejected claims that Maine's Sex Offender Registry was unconstitutional. The 16 plaintiffs (John Doe) argued that they should not be required to be on the registry because it was not part of their punishment and was added long after they had completed their sentence. Murphy wrote in her 70-page decision that *"the sting of injustice"* felt by the plaintiffs was understandable, but the judge went on to say that the legislature should have the power to pass laws for the public good. *"The court owes the legislature that deference under the balance of powers."*

Justice Murphy's decision is not the final word in this complicated legal scenario, in fact, her opinion merely sets the stage for the next step – an appeal of her ruling to the Maine Supreme Court where the final decision will be made. Everyone, including the Attorney General's Office, is anticipating the appeal because of the enormous impact this decision will have on the plaintiffs and the entire sex offender registry concept. It is likely the high court will not rule on the appeal until the middle of 2012.

This book presents a well thought out "Plan" that should be adopted and implemented by the legislature in the coming year. It will incorporate a workable and fair "tier system" as part of the sex offender registry. The specifics of the plan will appear in chapters 6 and 7, but a brief glimpse of some of the ingredients at this point might be interesting. These "tiers" provide guidance for the public and law enforcement agencies as to the potential risk level of sex offenders to society. This will be a new approach to the current concept of the Maine Sex Offender Registry and new a philosophy that partially avoids the existing problems of mixing low risk with the high-risk offenders as they appear on the registry for public viewing on the Internet. The plan also requires the use of "lay" terminology when describing the convictions on of the offenders on the registry versus the legal jargon currently used that only lawyers and judges understand. This change allows the average citizen to more clearly understand the crimes that were committed by the registrant. Enough of a peek ahead at what the plan looks like, but it's fair to say that there will be major changes proposed with substantial research to support the new direction.

Assigning a "potential risk to reoffend" to a sex offender who is being released from jail or prison is difficult and could put the state in jeopardy if not done carefully and consistently. How will the risk be defined? Will there be the creation of some type of super board of "experts" who will examine each individual case and determine, based on who knows what, the likelihood of the person reoffending? This obviously is problematic for reasons that will be examined in detail in the following chapters.

The plan provides another option that would determine the risk level of the offender. Such a determination can be based strictly on the actual conviction, e.g. rape: highest level of risk; incidental nudity in public: lowest level of risk. This would provide more consistency, but it might lack the component of true individual risk assessments. Regardless, it's the most practical approach and will be a basic component of the plan's purpose - making the registry more functional.

Other portions of the plan recommends ways, where appropriate, to coordinate Maine's sex offender laws with the newest federal law - the Adam Walsh Act (AWA). Another key part of the plan is the reorganization of the Computer Crimes Unit (CCU). The CCU is one of the best-kept secrets in Maine and is managed and run everyday (and night) by real heroes. The CCU is an amazing story that will; 1.) Inspire an appreciation of the unit's professional expertise, 2.) Provide an eye- opening revelation about the extraordinary procedures employed in locating children who are being sexually abused and recorded in videos and photographs on the Internet and, 3.) Chill you to your core because of the severity of the assaults on children that are often routine in the Unit's challenges every day.

The plan includes proposals and ideas based on this author's many years of experience in the sex offender legislative arena. Included are the ideas of many other professionals and experts who bring a wide range of practical knowledge and philosophical beliefs to what is a bold and exciting package of changes that are long over due.

CHAPTER 2

THE EASTER MURDERS
"HE DIDN'T SAY ANYTHING, HE JUST SHOT HIM IN COLD BLOOD!"

"HE TOOK whatever it was in that clip and put into my boy's body. (One of the bullets) blew out half of his teeth – there was a hole that goes right through (his face)," stated Shirley Turner as she recalled how her son was killed.

It was around 6:00 in the morning on Easter Sunday, April 16, 2006, Stephen Marshall knocked on William Elliott's trailer door. William and his live-in girlfriend heard the knock, but they were still in bed, so ignoring the early morning visitor was easy to do. William's mother said her son probably figured whomever it was, they would come back later at a more reasonable hour.

Little did William or his girlfriend know that Stephen Marshall would indeed come back to finish the job he had not yet completed on his carefully planned journey of justice. Approximately three hours earlier Marshall had shot and killed Joseph Gray who lived in Milo, Maine just 24 miles to the north. On this early morning Stephen was intent on murdering William Elliott, the second killing on this gruesome Sunday.

According to the autopsy report Joseph Gray moved to Milo where he lived with his wife, Janice, and her son, Brian, for three years before Gray's death. Joseph had been convicted of sexual assault against a child under the age of 14 in Massachusetts in 1992 prior to the creation of that state's sex offender registry. When Massachusetts's sex offender registry was created, Joseph was required to register there, and when he moved to Maine he was required to register in Maine. The autopsy report (f17) also stated that Joseph Gray had "been imprisoned for them (offenses)," however his wife, Janice, stated emphatically that Joseph never served time in prison. Janice's belief is that the court didn't consider Joseph dangerous and therefore agreed to a plea bargain that avoided any incarceration.

"He never spent one night in prison," she repeated several times during an interview in her home in Bradford, Maine, on August 21, 2011.

At the time of the shooting, the Gray's residence was located a short distance off Route 16 in Milo also known as West Main Street. The house is small in size with a garage connected to the main building facing a good size lawn and yard in the front. There is an extended view from the back of the house looking out towards Mount Katahdin making the entire property quite pleasant. As Janice said, "This was our dream house."

Even though it is named *Main Street* the property is located a distance away from the stores, businesses, and city buildings in downtown Milo. The house cannot be seen from the street (most Mainers would call it a road), because it sits well back from view with a long driveway that sort of meanders as it curves through the trees, first one way, then the other, on the way to the house. The mailbox is next to the road with the painted numbers *233* easily seen by anyone driving by looking for a house number. This, along with other evidence, indicates that Marshall was clearly looking for a predetermined address reaffirming the assumption that, in an effort to locate his target, Marshall had utilized Maine's sex offender registry, which provided a picture, an address, and a description (albeit in legalese) of Gray's offenses.

Interestingly, at the edge of the front lawn positioned next to an area with trees and bushes, is a high intensity lamp attached to a long (what most would call a telephone pole) pole similar to those seen along Maine roads that are used for the attachment of the usual telephone, electric, and cable wires. The autopsy report (f17) mentioned that this lamp was on at the time of the shooting and because of the brightness of the light it would have fully illuminated the yard in front of the house where Marshall would have entered on the way to secure the best position to locate and shoot Gray. Between the edge of the lawn and the front of the house there was nothing to conceal Marshall's movements, however having the advantage of being an unexpected intruder allowed him to maneuver through the lighted yard unnoticed. Joseph was sitting on his couch completely unaware of the deadly barrage of bullets soon to be fired at him from point blank range. (It should be noted that Janice Gray said that the high intensity light was not on having had it turned off several days earlier to save electricity). In either case, as noted, if Joseph and Janice were not expecting someone to walk through their yard, especially in the early morning hours, it wouldn't be difficult for Marshall to sneak up to the house below the sight line of people sitting in the living room either asleep or certainly not attentive to what's happening outside.

Janice returned from her job at the regular time around midnight and saw Joseph sleeping on the couch in front of the television. She said that Joe always waited up knowing she would be arriving after completing the usual work shift from 3–11 p.m. When Janice got home, both would usually talk about her workday and she would tell Joe all of the things that happened including her gripes that Joe listened to dutifully. Together they would watch television, especially Joe's favorite show, *The Forensic Files*, which, ironically, was the show both had watched that night. After watching two episodes of the "Files" Janice finished the ice cream she had gotten from the refrigerator and then decided to go to bed. Joe chose to stay up a while longer and watch a little more television with their dog, Max.

The large picture window, where Marshall assumed his attack position, provided an excellent viewpoint to observe Joseph dosing on the couch. Ironically, that same large window provided an unobstructed likewise view of the front yard, had Joe been inclined to look. Janice went to bed around 2 a.m. and was awakened by the dog barking at approximately 2:50 a.m. Marshall had knocked lightly on the door, not loud enough for the Grays to hear – but Max heard it. Marshall may have been trying to get Joseph's attention with the light knock without waking Janice. Janice got out of bed walked over to the front door located just a couple of feet from the picture window and looked out the door window expecting to see a deer or some other wild animal. Instead, Janice was struck with fear because there in the night stood a man (Marshall) positioned as if waiting for someone to open the door.

"When I saw him, horror strikes ... when it's 3 a.m. I jumped back and said to Joe that someone was at the door so he got half way into a standing position to go look to see who it was. I saw a spark (Janice's description of the flash in the dark caused by firing a gun), by the front window and saw Joe thrown back against the wall." Joe had been shot just below the left breast area and had landed back on the couch. Joe told Janice to call an ambulance then Janice saw more "sparks," by the window. She was able to crawl on the floor to the back of the couch and reach up for the phone that was on the wall. "I dialed 411 first by mistake and then got 911. They didn't believe me at first," Janice explained as she continued to recall the details of those horrible moments. "I was cowering behind the couch thinking he was going to pick me off too – one of the bullets hit the wall right by the phone where I was lying."

When Janice first saw Marshall as she peeked through the door window she noticed his position, Marshall was facing the door as if waiting for someone to open it. Then looking again she saw his back was towards the door and he was looking in the direction of the picture window to the left of the front door. There is a decorative stonewall, about three feet high, located under the picture window and near the top of the front door steps that encompasses a flower garden area. Marshall moved the short distance from the front steps onto the stonewall, thus providing a clear line of fire at Joseph and it was from that vantage point that Stephen Marshall began shooting.

As Joe fell back to the couch Marshall pumped five more bullets into him. The autopsy report described the following: "When the police arrived Joe was seated on the couch slumped slightly to the right with his hands in his lap. Directly in front of him was a table littered with various prescriptions, a radio, several empty glasses, a bottle of Seven Up and some bags and papers. There was a hole through one of the brown paper bags along with other bullet holes in other parts of the house." (f6)

One note of interest, according to Janice there was only one bullet hole in the picture window even though Marshall had fired seven times. It appears that he had such a steady hand that he held the gun in the same position and fired repeatedly at Gray without moving the end of the barrel of the gun in any significant way.

Several cigarette butts, all being of a Canadian brand, were found on the ground outside the window. Marshall probably stood in the yard for a long period of time for what purpose is unknown. Stephen could have been contemplating the upcoming task or he may have been waiting for Janice to go to bed. These types of questions will never be answered completely just as the many questions that haunt Janice Gray to this day will go unanswered.

When the police arrived they told Janice to stay in the kitchen and they went into the living room to examine Joseph's condition. "They came back to the kitchen and told me he was gone," she said. She went to the couch and looked at him and she said he didn't look like he was dead. "He had a little bit of blood coming out of his nose and mouth and I noticed the big (bullet) hole in the lower part of his chest area and so I put two fingers into the hole just so I would know for sure that he had been shot and was dead," she recalled.

Steven Marshall used a Ruger 45-caliber semi-automatic handgun to shoot Gray and Elliott that night and in both cases at least one of the bullets hit each victim in the mouth. The bullet that entered Gary's mouth passed through his head severing his brain from the base (medulla). The location of that shot alone would be instantly fatal. (f17)

Oddly enough, State Police Sgt. Steve Pickering, the officer investigating the killing of Joseph Gray, was still in Milo sitting in his cruiser discussing the situation with the medical examiner when the call about the Elliott shooting came in. From the description Pickering received on the phone, the Elliott murder involved the same caliber of gun and the method of attack was similar. It was immediately suspected at the time that given the initial circumstances both murders could have been committed by the same person and, of course, they were.

William Elliott lived in a trailer located at 953 Main Street in Corinth, Maine. Again, as with Gray's location in Milo, this section of Main Street is out in a more remote area away from the downtown business district and the usual perception of a "Main Street" once again does not apply. A more appropriate descriptive Maine term in this case would be "road" or even a highway. The trailer sits down well below the level of the road and the steep driveway goes directly from the road to the front of the trailer. There are low bushes and tall grass that extend along the outer shoulders of the road and on both sides of the entrance to the driveway, but once directly in front of the driveway the view of the trailer and surrounding area is clear. The steep, narrow driveway provides a limited area to maneuver a vehicle especially for the purposes of making a quick escape. It appears that Marshall parked his truck on the edge of the highway, which has a wide shoulder and plenty of room for traffic to pass undeterred by a parked vehicle. Traffic moves fast in this area, because it's more like a two lane highway - wide and straight with good visibility.

Once again, it wouldn't be evident, especially to a stranger, who lived in the undistinguishable house trailer in an obscure location. However, the number 953 on the mailbox was clearly visible, reinforcing the strong assumption that use of the address from the registry was again the primary tool for locating the victim.

Shirley recalled the scenario of that morning stating that Marshall returned to William's home at about 8:15, knocked again and this time William opened the door and Marshall "…. didn't say anything, he just shot him in cold blood. He shot him several times!" Turner said.

The autopsy, performed the day after the killing on April 17, 2006 by Dr. Marguerite DeWitt, MD, Deputy Chief Medical examiner for the State of Maine, stated, "*The deceased is supine in the hallway just off the front door to the trailer. That hallway is full of clutter as is the dooryard and the rest of the trailer. The deceased has obvious gunshot wounds to the head, chest and to his left great toe. There is also a wound on the dorsum of his left forearm, at the junction of the wrist with hand.*"(f7)

Marshall clearly had every intention of killing William, not just aiming to wound, as evidenced by both the number of times Marshall shot him – nine, and specifically where the bullets hit his target. The gunshot wounds included two in the face (mouth and jaw), one in the left thigh and four times in the chest/stomach area. Probably because of the commotion and intensity of the moment another shot randomly hit the left big toe and another in the left wrist. (f7) Shirley stated that she talked with William's girlfriend about the details of what happened immediately after the shooting stopped. "Anne came out of the bedroom to check on William, she saw Stephen (Marshall) standing over my son's body while he gurgled in his own blood. As Marshall left she chased him as he ran up towards his truck. (Stephen) did a U-turn and gestured to Anne with his hand shaped like a gun as to shoot at her then he jumped in his pickup and drove off."

From everything that the police could gather, it appeared that Marshall did search and find both Gray's and Elliott's names and addresses on the Maine sex offender registry and evidently was intent on killing them for reasons only Stephen knew. Marshall's intent was clear, and he certainly demonstrated proficient skills with a handgun by shooting each man in the mouth, which is not an easy target, especially given the circumstances.

It takes considerable skill to hit a small target with a handgun. This is true especially with emotions running high and raging adrenaline that must have been surging through Marshall's body and crazed mind at the moment he repeatedly pulled the trigger with speed and determination. If you think it's easy to hit any specified mark with a handgun, give it a try sometime. Try hitting a little area the size of a human mouth, for example, with a handgun – of course not a real mouth. The degree of difficulty will quickly be apparent, not to mention doing so under the high anxiety of that type of situation. It does enhance the theory by some who suggest that Marshall might have been sexually abused at some point in his life involving oral sex or something similar. When told during a telephone interview on October 21, 2011 with this author that Stephen had shot both Elliott and Gray in the mouth Margaret Miles, Stephen's mother, said she did not know that, but said, "[That] does not surprise me."

On Wednesday, April 12, 2006 Stephen Marshall, who lived in Cape Breton, Nova Scotia, headed to Houlton, Maine to visit his father, Ralph Marshall. It was reported by the Canadian Broadcasting Corporation in an article entitled, "Avenging Angel" that Ralph was expecting his son to come to Houlton and when Stephen's car broke down in Sackville, New Brunswick he called his father to come get him – and he did. (f8) Whether or not Ralph knew about his son's extended mission while in Maine is unknown. Stephen's mother, Margaret, said in the same telephone interview on October 21, 2011, that she believes Ralph was fully aware of Stephen's real purpose for going to Maine. She said that her former husband encouraged Stephen to be a gun enthusiast and to become proficient with handling and shooting guns and she felt Ralph influenced him to engage in violence.

Early Sunday morning, April 16, 2006, Stephen left his father's home in Houlton on his way to 233 Main Street in Milo, Maine. It was reported that he quietly sneaked out of the house through a window after stealing the keys to his father's pickup truck. In fact, Ralph reportedly called the Maine State Police to inform them that his truck and some guns were stolen from his house. Margaret believes differently and thinks that Ralph was fully aware of Stephen's departure and purpose as she said in the same telephone interview, "Stephen did not steal the (pickup truck) keys – his father gave them to him and he walked out the front door."

After Marshall's second killing he fled and later abandoned the truck in Bangor and jumped on a Vermont Bus Lines coach and headed for Boston. It didn't take long for law enforcement authorities to trace Stephen due to the license plate information provided by William Elliott's girl friend. When Massachusetts Bay Transit Authority police boarded the bus, Marshall, sitting 13 rows behind the driver, put the Colt 45 to his head and fired, killing himself instantly and in the process splattering five other passengers with his blood. (f9)

"Pedophiles are Worse than Murderers – They Kill your Soul!"

No one will ever know for certain why Stephen Marshall hunted down and killed William Elliott and Joseph Gray. Margaret believes that her son was sexually abused as a child and that the abuse significantly contributed to his unstable childhood. Margaret said at age 13 he became unmanageable so he was sent to live with his father in Idaho. The couple had separated when Stephen was 8 years old. He lived with his father for three years and Margaret feels it was during that time in Idaho that Stephen was sexually assaulted. "When he returned from Idaho he looked like a battle fatigued soldier," Margaret said as she described Stephen's change in appearance and attitude upon his return to Nova Scotia.

Margaret said she felt that something was wrong because of peculiar things he would do like, " when he would go to sleep he would cover his private parts with his hands."

People have developed various theories as to what motivated Stephen to use the sex offender registry to identify his victims. Margaret said in the telephone interview that he had strong feelings about sex offenders and she quoted him as saying to her a few weeks before the shootings, "Pedophiles are worse than murderers – they kill your soul."

Why select William Elliott and why Joseph Gray? Was it because they were available or for some other reason? One clue is worthy of mentioning. According to Margaret Miles, Stephen had a Bible that he read regularly because, she said, "He found Christ," and "In that Bible," Margaret says, "there were several underlined passages in the Book of Corinthians." History tells us that Corinth was the most influential and prosperous city in Greece between 350 and 250 B.C. and was located at the crossroads of international trade resulting in the mingling of all kinds of people, ideas and morals. The reputation for having a variety of sexual practices in the city was widespread so much that a Greek author coined a new Greek verb *"corinthianize"* that meant "to participate in immoral sexual practices." Archaeological evidence suggests homosexual activity was thriving in the city. (f10) Another historian around 7 B.C. told of a thousand temple prostitutes plying their trade in Corinth and he quoted an old proverb laced with sarcasm that suggested, "Not every man is man enough to go to Corinth."

Gray and Elliott were just two of 34 sex offenders that Marshall had researched on Maine's online sex offender registry. (f11) He evidently went to homes of other registered sex offenders, but for some reason decided to kill just the two. Other potential targets might not have been home, or there may have been other distractions like dogs or neighbors in close proximity. No one will ever know. What is known is that William was at home in Corinth as was Joseph in Milo – in plain sight as easy targets.

William Ellliott was convicted in 2002 in Newport District Court of sexual abuse of a minor and served approximately six months and was required to register as a sex offender for 10 years. William's case is one that begs for a change in the registry, a change that distinguishes between high and low risk offenders. William Elliott was not a predator. In fact, the girl he had been seeing and was convicted of sexually abusing, according to Shirley Turner, actually came to William's trailer one day and asked if she could stay with him. Shirley said that based on discussions with her son she was certain they had consensual sex that was short lived since Rose was only with William for a day or two.

The day the girl arrived at the trailer, William called his mother to ask for advice since the recently arrived young girl was two weeks away from reaching the critical age (in this case) of 16 and engaging in sexual acts, albeit consensual, would be illegal. Shirley said to him, "Now wait a minute, William, maybe you should wait and he said to me, but she wants to have sex and I said wait a minute, you should think about this."

William refused to make the girl leave because as he emphatically stated to Shirley, "Mom I want to marry this girl." According to Shirley, when the girl returned home a day or two later and her parents learned what had happened they filed charges against William. He signed a confession which was part of the plea agreement, served the required time in jail and under Maine law was required to register on the Maine sex offender registry, but for only 10 because of the nonviolent nature of the offense. The Maine sex offender registry has just two categories in terms of severity of offense. Registrants must be listed on the sex offender registry either for life for having committed the most serious sexual offenses or for 10 years for having committed what is considered a less serious crime. However, it should be noted that some of the 10-year registrants can be considered a risk to society as well.

"Without the registry, he'd still be alive today."

The Sex Offender Registry serves a useful purpose, but there are significant problems that need to be addressed. For example, when an ordinary citizen looks at the registry it is difficult for them (based on the presented descriptions) to distinguish between a registrant who may pose a greater risk of reoffending from a registrant who poses a less of a risk. The average citizen cannot tell the sexually violent predators on the registry from those who may have had consensual sex with a minor or they had committed some other "low risk" offense like peeing in public, (this law was recently changed removing the simple act of public urination as offense requiring registration).

The Joseph Telliers and William Elliotts are on opposite ends of the spectrum in terms of risk to society. The State and the legislature have not given this deficiency in the registry the appropriate attention, partly because of insufficient funding. The sex offender registry is a useful tool, but until it is fixed this "tool" can be as deadly as the nine Colt 45 bullets fired into the body of William Elliott. As Shirley said, "Without the registry, he'd still be alive today."

Shirley is quick to explain that William was very intelligent and had a high I.Q. However, he had Asperger's Syndrome that made it difficult for him to socialize and communicate effectively with others. William's disability manifested itself in the difficulty to be accepted by peers and explained his desire to be self-employed, which fit well with his decision to be a junk dealer. The area surrounding his trailer was evidence of that trade, cluttered with vehicle parts, tires and other discarded items. William had dreams of owning a "100 acres of land," expanding the junk business and "marrying the girl he loved and having a lot of kids," as his mother tells it. William's mental disability was probably a factor in his decision to become sexually involved with a girl he loved. She had come to him asking for caring and support, something he had not experienced often. He felt quite clumsy in social situations, especially with the opposite sex. Understandably, turning this girl away was not a realistic option, something he could not easily do – so he didn't.

No one knows what was going through the mind of Stephen Marshall or the demons he was dealing with while planning his Easter rampage. However, one could argue that had William's crime been described on the sex offender registry in more understandable terminology then things might have been different. At least Marshall would have known that William Elliott was not a pedophile who preyed on innocent children and wasn't a deviant child molester and was on the registry mostly because of a deficient and broken sex offender registration and notification law. Marshall might never have knocked on that trailer door in Corinth, Maine, not once - but twice, had he understood the full extent of William's crime. William is one example of how just being on the sex offender registry, regardless of the reasons and the individual circumstances, one can be perceived as evil. In fact, relatively speaking, William was quite innocent in terms of being a sexual predator and certainly did not deserve to be murdered in cold blood.

There is a definite need to properly educate the general public, as well as our elected officials about the deficiencies of the sex offender registry. Most everyone agrees that those listed on the sex offender registry are seen as the scum of society, perverts who are literally waiting in the shadows to snatch our children or sexually assault our daughters and wives.

A visit to the website, http://sor.informe.org/sor/ will probably leave you with an uneasy sense of evilness, even repulsion. Take a look and then describe your feelings. Just looking at the mug shots of these offenders gives the quintessential image of what a sexual predator looks like. Add to that the inability to translate the legalese describing the offenses of the registrants in more understandable terms, and you have the final ingredient for the intangible uneasiness emitted by the registry. The truth of the matter is that the registry includes those who have committed serious and heinous felonies and others who committed misdemeanors. People like Joseph Tellier and William Elliott are included on the registry without distinction to the average person or to those who are intent on vigilantism.

Shirley Turner had a very difficult life, as she explains it, starting at age 5 when she was sexually molested on a regular basis. She said the abuse went from being fondled to being forced to have intercourse by the time she was 13. Shirley said her mother was physically abused over the years as well. Obviously, the lives of both Shirley and her mother were tragic in many ways. What happened next one might expect would occur in the back mountains of some southern state, but not in the civilized world of the twentieth century.

AS They Say – You Can't Make This Stuff Up!

Shirley explained that the family moved from Maine to Florida and one day Shirley said her mother actually witnessed her being sexually abused and became extremely upset. Shirley said her mother and stepfather were divorced and her stepfather left and took Shirley with him. This is where things really got weird. On December 13, 1979, Shirley said she and her stepfather were married in Darlington, South Carolina –she was only 17 years old and he was 35.

According to Shirley, her birth certificate was altered so her birth date appeared as October 22, 1961, instead of the correct year 1962. The alteration of her certificate allowed the illegal marriage to be performed.

So, the stepfather's stepdaughter becomes the stepfather's wife and what would have been his step-grandson is now his *son* - William.

William Elliott was born on July 10, 1981 at Eastern Maine Medical Center, in Bangor, Maine. Shirley was 19 years old. From the time Shirley was 6 months pregnant until William was 3 months old they, lived in a tent in the Maine woods about ¼ mile from the nearest water supply. In order to give the baby a warm bath Shirley would heat water in soda bottles in their old car. All three slept on the ground which caused Shirley to develop back problems that she still suffers from today. By October it was getting very cold especially when living outside in those conditions. Wayne decided to get a job at the tannery in Hartland because, as Shirley said, he was afraid the State would take the baby if they found out that they were living in the woods. Both Shirley and William had difficult starts in life, but one survived and one didn't. With the appropriate changes to the sex offender registry perhaps a few needless tragedies like William's murder can be prevented.

As discussed earlier, once a person is placed on the registry, his or her reputation, once placed on the registry, is ruined regardless of the reason for placement. Once on the registry, a person's life can become a constant nightmare perhaps deserved in some cases but not in others. Society does not tolerate sex offenders, and being part of that infamous group, subjects the registrants to people's worst fears and highest levels of disgust and scorn. Making general assumptions about many on the registry would be fair and just. However, for just as many others it is not only unfair and unjust – it can be deadly.

Added Years in Prison – Worth it!

To illustrate just how dangerous and destructive appearing on the registry can be, look at the cases where extraordinary steps are taken by the accused to stay off the registry. More defense attorneys and defendants are now realizing that placement on the registry should be avoided at all costs. Plea bargains involving sex offenses, especially the misdemeanor sexual abuse crimes, often result in the defendant accepting longer sentences or other greater penalties in exchange for not having to register on the sex offender registry after release from prison.

"I would have been in the same category with pedophiles and rapists." Those are the words of Nathaniel Sargent who accepted a four-year sentence for aggravated assault – a felony - if the prosecutor would drop the misdemeanor charge of sexual abuse of a minor that would have included registration on the sex offender registry.

Sargent was 21 and dated a 14-year-old for about three weeks, according to statements made to the *Bangor Daily News*. The sex was consensual, but he realized that the situation would be nothing but trouble. Even though Sargent removed himself from the relationship, the girl's parents still filed charges. Just before the trial began, Sargent's attorney worked the plea bargain that resulted in a much lengthier sentence for a felony charge, if the State would drop the sexual abuse of a minor charge. His attorney, Jeffrey Toothaker, as reported in the same *Bangor Daily News* article, was clear about the dangers associated with the sex offender registry. Toothaker said, "It's one conviction fits all, we really should be grading them and deciding who poses the biggest threat." (f12)

Amen!

Where did the sex offender registry come from?

In October 1989, in his hometown of St. Joseph, Minnesota, 11-year-old Jacob Wetterling was abducted at gunpoint by a masked man. Jacob and his younger brother, Trevor, and another boy, were coming home from a convenience store when Jacob was taken. The gunman told Trevor and his friend to run into the woods or he would shoot them. *Despite national press coverage along with extensive searching by family and law enforcement, Jacob still has not been found – it has been 21 years.* (13)

As a result of Jacob's abduction, in 1994 Congress passed the **Jacob Wetterling Crimes Against Children and Sexually Violent Offender**

Registration Act that was part of the Violent Crime Control and Law Enforcement Act. The law mandated all states to "to implement a sex offender registry" requiring released sex offenders to provide their home and work addresses along with personal information to local law enforcement agencies. This new federal law, that became known as the "Jacob Wetterling Act," was an attempt by Congress to create a managed list of convicted and released sex offenders in each state that would assist law enforcement agencies in monitoring these known offenders. The assumption in the Jacob Wetterling abduction case was that the perpetrator was most likely a pedophile with possibly a history of sex offenses against children. Therefore, by requiring each state to have their own sex offender registry, police could keep an eye on the known sex offenders, thus reducing the chances of repeated abductions and sexual assaults on children. The theory sounded good, but making such assumptions is not a reliable foundation for making laws.

This was the national birth of sex offender registries created as a result of a tragic event involving a young child whose loss was something that everyone could identify with and that caused instant outrage and public demand for justice. Everyone has a young relative, friend or neighbor who just as easily could have been Jacob. As you would expect, the outcry by the public was that of frustration, fear and disbelief that such a thing could happen. What followed was also expected. Elected officials tried to be out front on the issue, showing the same concern, frustration and compassion by sponsoring and passing a new law aimed at preventing such a tragedy from happening again. To politicians it is important to be seen as taking action – doing something, anything - even though the public may be better served by proceeding more slowly and carefully examining the causes and consequences of proposed new laws before passing them and then, and only then, moving forward to construct a possible legislative solution. Politicians, by their very nature, do what they think the voters want and expect, even if their actions are shortsighted and more reactionary than logical. Not acting is considered weak and uncaring and lacking leadership. The media and press also want to be seen as being "on top of the story" when a tragedy happens and that means, in the case of child sexual assaults, going to the local legislators and essentially asking, "What are you going to do about this?" To a Senator or Representative that's too tempting and ego-massaging to ignore. Such a question demands a quick response outlining a plan and solution. After all that is what is expected, and it means more television, radio and newspaper interviews and, of course, reelection.

The now famous - or "infamous" – national sex offender registry system was created. Soon after adoption of the Wetterling Act, more federal laws followed, each appearing "tougher" than the previous law. This piece-meal approach – all based on emotion and political swagger – ended up creating a series of federal laws that are so far reaching that most states are not practically or financially able to comply with them.

Following adoption of the Jacob Wetterling Act, two years later in 1996 Congress amended that law by enacting what is now known as "Megan's Law" which added "community notification" to the sex offender registration requirement. Once again, it was the horrific death of one young child that resulted in this new law.

Seven-year-old Megan Kanka lived in Mercer County, New Jersey, and was raped and murdered by Jesse Timmendequas, a sex offender who had previously been convicted of sex crimes and lived across the street from Megan with other sex offenders. This new law, "Megan's Law," which was passed in an incredibly short period of time by the New Jersey General Assembly, was a compilation of seven bills that "required sex offenders to register with and be tracked by the state, required that communities be notified of sex offenders' addresses and required that conviction for a second sexual assault required life imprisonment."

Then came the Jessica Lunsford Act, which was quickly drafted, passed and signed into law by then Florida Governor, Jeb Bush in May of 2005 after Jessica Lunsford was kidnapped, raped and murdered by a convicted sex offender. This new Florida law set a minimum of a 25-year sentence for anyone convicted of sexually abusing or preying on a child under the age of 12. It also required satellite tracking of sex offenders in Florida for the first time. This law became model legislation for many other states that passed similar laws that became known around the country as "Jessica's Law." Even though it wasn't a federal law the results were similar.

The sex offender registry was created and then transformed into a complex conglomerate with pieces added each time there was a heinous act against a child. In summary, it goes like this: the federal government started with the Wetterling Act creating the registry, then Megan's Law requiring community notification, followed by Jessica's Law adding a 25-year minimum sentence and tracking (Maine did not adopt that law), and now the latest federal law and the mother of them all, the Adam Walsh Act, the details of which I will share with you in a later chapter. Many states are still trying to comply with this complex and costly new law that was named after the son of the well-known host of the television show, "America's Most Wanted," John Walsh. His 6-year-old son, Adam, was kidnapped and murdered in 1981. Like all of the previous laws mentioned, we have one more law based on a specific tragedy. A good rule of thumb to follow is this: If a law is named after someone, especially a child, be suspicious, at least regarding the amount of due deliberation and careful thought given to its creation.

Maine's Sex Offender Registry – At Least it Started Out Right

"Pooch came to my house one night, sat down in the chair and said he had just arrested a guy who had been molesting a little girl. He said she was very scared and terrified. Pooch said if he had only known (this guy's history) and that he was in town he could have been on the look out and maybe could have saved that little girl from the terrible abuse she experienced," said Anne Haskell. She was recalling the night that Wayne "Pooch" Drown, police officer in the Town of Gorham, Maine came to her house with a heavy burden on his shoulders.

Anne Haskell was then State Representative Anne Larrivee and was serving her second term in the Maine House of Representatives representing the town of Gorham. (Following the death of her husband, Anne has since remarried and now lives in Portland, Maine, where once again she was elected to the Maine House of Representatives representing part of Portland.)

Pooch and Anne knew each other quite well as she had been a local Town Councilor in Gorham and had worked with the police department on a variety of local issues. Pooch was very comfortable talking with Anne so it wasn't uncommon for him to share concerns with her. Coming to the Larrivee house for such a purpose wasn't unusual, but according to Anne, the depth of Pooch's despair for the little girl and the frustration of not being able to help or prevent her from continuing to be abused in such a heinous way had clearly gotten to him. "I could see it in his eyes – the hurt and helplessness. He didn't come to me because he wanted me to do something as much as he just wanted to share his feelings," Anne recalled about that night.

Officer Drown was well known in town and, according to Anne, he was well liked especially by the teenagers and by those who might find themselves caught in some mischievous activities. "The kids kind of grew up with Pooch and they would quickly confess to him when they did something that they knew was wrong," Anne said. Police officers can evoke fear and even hate among the teenage crowd, but Pooch was different. He respected the kids and used the police authority in a positive way that made the kids trust him.

Realizing that Pooch's experience was probably not an uncommon circumstance, Anne decided that something should be done by way of a law that would at least require notification to local law enforcement agencies when a convicted sex offender lived in their community. Anne wrote and submitted Maine's first sex offender registry law two years *before* the federal law (Jacob Wetterling Act) was passed. Anne's bill was designed to be workable and deliberate, not attention getting. It just focused on providing a tool for the law enforcement agencies to help them in their efforts to protect everyone – adults and children alike.

As a result of Representative Larrivee's diligence, the Maine Legislature passed its first law in 1992 (PL1991, c.809) requiring registration of sex offenders, (for 15 years), who were convicted of gross sexual assault against victims who were less than 16 years old at the time of the offense. The law applied to anyone sentenced on or after June 30, 1992. As of September 1, 2011 there were 2934 active registrants on Maine's Sex Offender Registry. Of those, 640 must register for 10 years and the remaining 2294 are required to register for life. (f3)

That's how Maine got its first sex offender registry: a well-crafted law that, unfortunately over the following 18 years, became twisted with unrealistic expectations, cumbersome regulations and too many federal interventions resulting in unintended consequences that were often unworkable and occasionally fatal.

William Elliott and Joseph Gray are two cases that need to be reviewed and dissected carefully in an effort to identify some of the specific problems within the Maine sex offender registry system that need to be addressed sooner rather than later. The current system is broken and the public deserves a clear explanation of the existing problem areas and the confidence that it can be fixed. There will always be a delicate line separating the goal of protecting the innocent while pursuing the evil. The evil are usually easy to identify; the innocent may be known as well. But there are often others, invisible at the outset, who are swept up in the consequences of legislative "good intentions" and become victims themselves. Just ask Janice and Shirley.

CHAPTER 3

SEX OFFENDERS HAVE MANY DISGUISES

THE UNITED States Department of Justice reports only 13 percent of new sex crimes are committed by known sex offenders and that such crimes are at least six times more likely to be committed by other types of offenders who do not appear on any sex offender registry. (f14)

"So what did he do with his penis?" Marie remembered that horrible question as she sat in a courtroom alone with four men all staring and waiting for her response. Sitting in that morose, echo-filled chamber at that dreadful moment was "John," the man who had been sexually molesting Marie for the past two years, "John's" lawyer, the judge, and the lawyer that Marie's mother had hired when she finally realized that her husband had been sexually molesting Marie. There they were -- the all male quartet. The four men that seemed like a team facing one little girl named Marie. The question from "John's" lawyer seemed to bounce off the walls of the hollow room forever. "I was only 11 years-old and I was so ashamed and embarrassed sitting there with these men and as hard as I tried I couldn't answer the question. Inside I was screaming the answer, but nothing would come out. My mouth wouldn't work – I was so scared and frustrated too," Marie recalled. She was so terrified that she was unable to tell the judge about the horrible things that man had actually done with his penis and with his hands and fingers, for the past two years, so the story detailing the horrors that Marie had lived through went unsaid and the accused child molester walked away a free man.

Marie was born in 1965 and during the first years of her life she and her parents lived in Maine. A few years later her parents were divorced and when Marie was 9-years-old her mother married "John," a local police officer who worked for a police department in central Maine. Following the marriage the three of them immediately moved from Maine to a mid-western state, eventually settling in the quintessential small-town America.

"At first ["John"] would just tickle me and it was all quite innocent. Then while he was tickling, his hands would wander. Then he started fondling me and there was a lot of touching and probing in my genital area. I remember him saying that this is what he does to all of his girls," Marie recalled. He moved from tickling to more direct sexual contact by making Marie masturbate him and also making her perform oral sex on him. Marie remembers, "feeling so ashamed and I knew that if I did what he wanted I could then leave and he would leave me alone." Of course, that worked only until the next time. When "John" finished with Marie sometimes she would go outside and play, but she would dress in peculiar ways, like wearing her clothes inside out hoping someone would notice that everything was *not* okay. Marie was only a child and struggling to get someone – anyone - to hear her quiet pleading for help. It was difficult and frustrating for this little girl to carry such a burden. Why can't someone see me? Why can't someone help me?

"John" eventually got a job as the town's only police officer. He *was* the police department, which was not unusual for small towns in the mid-west. As time went on he was not only accepted by the townspeople, but actually became adored, even idolized by some, which was confusing to Marie and just didn't seem right. Marie, her mother and "John" lived the part of the idea family, having a house on Main Street across from the Dairy Queen and just down the street from the local church that they attended 4 or 5 times a week and ... where "John" was a *deacon*. He even wrote a column in the local newspaper about helping teens. Everyone looked up to him – except Marie, who knew all too well that this "respected man" was really someone who made her do things that caused her belly to hurt inside. Marie remembers how this man, the perceived perfect stepfather, told her repeatedly not to tell anyone about what they did or, "I'll hurt you and your mother." These words sent waves of fear through Marie's mind and body. She now realizes those words were nothing more than the controlling and intimidation tactics used skillfully and methodically by child molesters, to manipulate their victims.

Who would have guessed that this upstanding community leader, who was also a policeman, would be sexually molesting his little 9-year-old stepdaughter, not just once or twice, but repeatedly. For an abused, young child this was a "perfect storm." The clouds of intimidation were strategically placed in plain view for his victim to see and feel. "John" had the ultimate disguise: he was a highly respected cop and church leader in the community and his victim was available for personal pleasures 24 hours a day – part of the perfect family. "John" demanded his "special" attention and each time, after achieving his gratification, put his police uniform back on and walked out the door to his admiring flock of believers. Transformed, once again, back to the trusted and respected community leader everyone believed in – they would never believe anything different. Even after the two years of assaults were discovered, and an attempted prosecution was initiated, "John's" perfect storm prevailed when the efforts to seek justice had to be dropped. Perhaps even more frustrating was the fact that this beloved community leader was perceived by the people as the *victim* of lies by "that girl and her mother" and as a result enjoyed an even higher level of admiration and, from some, even pity. A perfect ending -- for "John."

Studies show that most sex offenders prey on family members, friends or acquaintances. Unfortunately, most sex offenders are never caught, and of those who are identified, only a very few are ever successfully prosecuted.

An Assistant Attorney General in the Maine Attorney General's office explained how few sex offenders are actually caught and convicted. She illustrated it as follows: Think of a large **V** shaped design. The distance between the two top points of the **V** represents the large number of people who are sexually molesting children. Half way down the V, that distance represents a much lower number – those who are discovered to be molesting children. Down in the very bottom of the **V**, that distance represents the smallest number - those who are actually convicted of their crime. And, only a percentage of those convicted are incarcerated. So when comparing the large population of actual sexual offenders to the number that are finally successfully prosecuted – the number is discouraging and alarming.

Marie's two-year hell with her stepfather is a prime example of how an alleged sex offender can commit the perfect crime and not only get away with it, but end up with the full support of his neighbors and friends in the community. In spite of Marie's horrible experience she survived and grew into a confident and well-adjusted woman. Marie's story is so common and yet in some ways so unique that it should be made into a movie so the public could better understand how sex offenders operate and how their victims can survive ...sometimes.

Most Sex Offenders are Around Us Everyday - Unnoticed

Joseph J. Tellier *was not* on Maine's Sex Offender Registry (until the Maine Legislature made the law retroactive in 2005) and he clearly should have been. William Elliott *was* on the sex offender registry and probably should *not* have been. "John" was never convicted as a sex offender or put on a registry and obviously *should have been*.

Like many who lived through abusive childhoods, Marie says that she has often thought about pursuing "John," but the cost for attorneys and the time involved always seemed to be too much of a hurdle. At one point she did employ a lawyer to locate and investigate the possibility of pressing charges against him, but again found that the cost could be significant. However, through various efforts Marie was able to find a recent address for him. Regardless of where he may be today, Marie still remembers his words that echo in her head, "I do this to all of my girls." She sadly wonders how many other little victims suffered from similar sexual attacks by "John" and how many more potential victims there are in his future!

As would be expected, Marie feels strongly that prosecution is certainly deserved in this case and her attorneys have indicated that even now, as an adult, she could very well be successful given today's intolerance toward child sex abusers. There are ways. She would at least like to have the opportunity to confront him as a confident woman rather than as the innocent little girl who was confused and so scared that she could not even speak to tell the judge at that critical moment all the unforgiveable things he did to her with his penis. Confrontation could be gratifying and maybe productive, not only in this case, but also in others where the offenders walk away from their victims without experiencing any consequences while at the same time leaving in their wake memories coated with indelible scars. Bitter memories of a stolen childhood continue to swirl just below the surface and can reappear without warning, stealing moments even to this day.

Other Disguises Used By Those Who Prey on the Innocent

Sex offenders and those who buy, sell and collect child pornography come in many shapes, colors and sizes. There are no boundaries as sexual assaults are committed by some of the most prominent people in society who are well known and trusted. Other sexual predators can be equally invisible because on the surface they appear as average, everyday citizens like the local business owner or a teacher or as we know all too well, a priest, minister or some other religious leader. Unfortunately, most sex offenders have such great disguises they would not be suspected of such a terrible offense like molesting and sexually assaulting children.

One of the more shocking revelations in Maine's history was the recent arrest and then conviction of James M. Cameron, who held a powerful position as a top drug prosecutor in the Maine Attorney General's Office. On August 23, 2010 Cameron was found guilty of 13 counts of sending, receiving and possessing child pornography over the Internet. Besides the images of child pornography, investigators found explicit images, emails, chats and other evidence on Cameron's four computers seized from his home. He was frequently missing from the office. Most believed he was working at home. Come to find out, working at home included being involved in online child porn activities. In fact, Cameron was gone from his AG's office so frequently there was a joke that made the rounds where someone would ask, "Where in the world is Jim Cameron?"(f15)

Some people may question why possessing and sharing child pornography is such a serious issue or certainly why it rises to the same level of seriousness as sexual molestation and assault. Online child pornography is reported to be one of the most lucrative industries in the world and the pornographers rely on using little children to be photographed and video taped while being sexually assaulted and sexually tortured in an infinite number of ways. As horrific as it sounds, kids are also used in "snuff" films, in which a child is filmed while being raped and tortured until the child actually dies or, if necessary, the scene ends by killing the child. In 2000, Britain was a key link in the biggest ever, (at that time), international investigation into the production and supply of pedophile "snuff" movies. A 30-year-old former car mechanic in Moscow, Russia was found to have produced and distributed the films that investigators discovered showed children dying while being sexually abused. In some cases, customers specifically requested films of child or infant killings. One senior customs officer who was involved in confiscating the films was quoted as saying, "We have seen some very, very nasty stuff involving sadistic abuse of very young children, but actual deaths on film takes it a whole step further. That is very worrying!"(f16)

Among the suspects of those who were purchasing the films were businessmen, public employees and a university student. Several of them were married, with children of their own. The investigation, which extended to the countries of Italy, Germany, Britain, and Russia, resulted in the seizure of huge quantities of pornographic material along with the lists of clients. It was revealed that covert film of young children naked or undressing was known as "SNIPE" video. The most appalling category was code-named "Necros Pedro," in which children were killed during or following the violent sexual assault. Many customers repeatedly ordered videos from the Russian who made the films in his small flat in Moscow's rundown Vykhino district. The Naples newspaper, Il Mattino, published a transcript of an alleged email between a prospective client and the Russian vendors that read as follows:

"Relax, I can assure you this one really dies," the Russian responds.
"The last time I paid and I didn't get what I wanted."
"What do you want?"
"To see them die." (16)

This is just one example of what happens on a regular basis to children. Even though the assaults are committed on the world stage, it is essentially minimized and kept from the public. Why? Too graphic? Makes us too uncomfortable? Makes us feel guilty that we are not aggressively working to stop the abuse? This is the kind of stuff that provides the sexual gratification for many twisted and deranged people who continue to want more "fresh" subjects to watch as their motivation for masturbation and as they engage in extremely bizarre sexual activities. Studies show that up to 80% of those who possess and share child pornography will eventually participate in the actual act of molesting a child. It is time the media and law enforcement agencies reveal to the public the details of these crimes and it is time for the rest of us to stand up and insist that more be done to protect the children.

There will be more in another chapter regarding the serious consequences of participating in and therefore supporting this illegal industry that relies on children, some still in diapers, to satisfy perverted sexual desires.

In spite of the fact that James Cameron's conviction did not include any evidence that he was directly involved in the sexual assault of children, the conviction was important in that it removed a high profile supporter and financial contributor to this underground, depraved cult. To have someone with Cameron's law enforcement credentials involved in illegal child pornography is, well – stunning to say the very least. Yet, once again it illustrates the fact that sex offenders most often are not the creepy looking guy everyone imagines wearing a trench coat peering at little children from behind a tree, but more likely someone who has the trust of family, friends and co-workers, which is, of course, the best disguise of all. (Note: In August of 2011 James Cameron was released on bail pending an appeal of his conviction. He was prosecuted by the U.S. Attorney's Office and at the time of this writing was waiting for the First Circuit Judge to decide on the appeal, which reportedly could result in one of the following options; a new trial; overturning of the conviction; or, denial of the appeal.)

Even a Kindergarten Teacher

Rob Mocarsky, who taught kindergarten in Jackman, Maine pleaded guilty to producing child pornography that depicted his kindergarten students in sexually explicit poses *in the classroom*. The children were made to pose in sexually suggestive ways similar to what you would see in adult magazines like Playboy, except these were not adult models. He had the students posing in French maid uniforms and other sexually suggestive clothing. These were 5 year-old children, which makes it chilling, repulsive and outrageous to most people. Mocarsky was arrested on January 6, 2011, at his home where the state police seized his personal computer that contained hundreds of images of these young children.

The investigation began after a parent notified the school about an incident involving her 5-year-old daughter. The parent said that Mocarsky had the girl remain in the classroom while the other students went to gym class. As was reported in the *Portland Press Herald,* it was at that time when Mocarsky took inappropriate, sexually suggestive photos of the little girl. Having 5 and 6 year old children pose in sexually provocative ways is even more horrifying when you realize what the specific motivations are for those who purchase and share these types of pictures. According to Federal Judge John Woodcock, Jr., Mocarsky did not distribute the images on the Internet; however, had he not been arrested the photos could have become part of online sharing of child pornography known as "peer-to-peer networking." A detailed explanation of child porn sharing is presented in Chapter 5, which is an inside view of how the child porn industry has developed a worldwide network of child porn users and supporters. Online sexual gratification is achieved through a variety of venues and the children used as the "stars" are innocent, unwilling and unsuspecting participants who face extreme danger every day unless they are rescued.

Mocarsky began teaching in 2002 at Forest Hills Consolidated School in Jackman. It is one of those rare schools that can still be found in rural areas that serve students in kindergarten through 12th grade. (f17) Once again, Mocarsky was not just the average kindergarten teacher, which by itself would suggest legitimacy and trustworthiness. This was someone who was even more above reproach and suspicion due to his unique background. Rob Mocarsky was a previous winner of the national Milken Family Foundation Award for Excellence in teaching. This is a very prestigious award that would be impressive to an interviewing school board during the hiring process and understandably supported by the community. To add more to his impressive resume' there was reportedly a photo taken at the time of the presentation of the award showing Mocarsky being congratulated by U. S. Senator Olympia Snowe. What better credentials could a person have when applying for a teaching job? What better credentials for a disguise?

On November 8, 2011 Mocarsky was sentenced to 16 years in prison followed by 10 years of supervised release, a condition requiring extensive monitoring by law enforcement officials. Judge Woodcock said, "You chose to teach kindergarten where you knew your students would be particularly naïve, trusting, eager to please and susceptible to suggestions. Your crime mandates a severe punishment."

Fortunately, Mocarsky was discovered *before* he did more than take inappropriate photos of kindergarten children. Who knows what else this award winning kindergarten teacher had planned.

If All Else Fails – Hypnotize Them

When she was just 12 years old this soon to be sexual abuse victim began hypnotism treatments to help break the bad habit of biting her fingernails. The hypnotist was Aaron Patton, 37, of Jay, Maine, who played minor roles in several major motion pictures and on television. In January 2011, he was found guilty on four counts of gross sexual assault and two counts of sexual abuse of a minor and of unlawful sexual contact against the young girl.

Now a 17-year-old, the girl testified that Patton began touching her breasts and private parts and two years later when the girl was 14 she testified that he took her into his bedroom and they had sex in front of a mirror so they could both watch. She told the court that she and Patton were having sex about once a week including anal and oral sex and after each sex session the girl said he would hypnotize her so that she would feel more relaxed and comfortable about their sexual encounters.

Patton's argument was that the girl was 16 when he was having sex with her, but the jury didn't buy that attempt to beat the charge. When police searched his apartment they found lingerie that he had bought for the young girl, along with sex aids and a copy of the publication, "Sex and Hypnosis." (f18)

Patton is appealing his conviction.

A High Profile Football Coach

He has not been proven guilty and his trial has not begun as of the writing of this chapter, but one of the most prominent and highly acclaimed college football coaches was recently charged with multiple counts of sexual abuse of young boys. Former Penn State defensive coordinator Jerry Sandusky was formerly charged on November 5, 2011, of involuntary deviate sexual intercourse, corruption of minors, endangering the welfare of a child, indecent assault and unlawful contact with a minor, as well as single counts of aggravated indecent assault and attempted indecent assault.

According to an article written by the Associated Press in the *Portland Press Herald* on November 6, 2011, the allegations against Sandusky range from sexual touching to oral and anal sex. Testimony at the grand jury hearings indicated the victims were in their early teens and younger when the offenses occurred.(f2) Penn State's reputation as a national football powerhouse is well known and Sandusky was the defensive guru who contributed significantly to the program's success. Joe Paterno, the long time, legendary, football coach at Penn State, was one of the best-known college coaches in the nation. Big time college football power and influence obviously played a key role in keeping these alleged eyewitness reports undercover for 15 years or longer.

The primary concern above all else should be the victims, if these multiple allegations are found to be true, and not about how the university or the football program might suffer. Maureen Dowd, columnist for the New York Times, wrote in an article published November 8, 2011, (f38), about the charges made by the Pennsylvania attorney general that Mike McQueary, a graduate student assistant coach, testified that he went into the locker room one Friday night and heard rhythmic slapping noises. He looked into the showers and saw a naked boy about 10 years old "with his hands up against the wall being subjected to anal intercourse by a naked Sandusky," according to the grand jury report. He reportedly told his father and coach Paterno the following day.

Dowd reported that the grand jury records included testimony that a janitor saw Sandusky performing oral sex on a boy in the showers and told his supervisor, who did not report it. As was reported in the *Portland*

Press Herald (f2), the Pennsylvania Attorney General Linda Kelly called Sandusky, "a sexual predator who used his position within the university and community to repeatedly prey on young boys. "

Powerful people in powerful positions protect themselves first. That is a fact. One of the most prominent university coaching dynasties in the country allegedly looked the other way as young boy after young boy was repeatedly sexually molested over the years. What was so important about protecting the football program at the university? As Dowd reported in the same article "Penn State rakes in $70 million a year from its football program." Enough said.

Not only do powerful people have the best disguises – they also have the best protectors. Once again sexually abused children were allegedly tossed in the rubble with other disposable incidentals for the purpose of maintaining a culture of fame, money, and power that was valued above all else – even the welfare of innocent sexually abused children. The good news – once the public and the media learned about the grand jury testimony pertaining to the abuse, the outrage followed and resulted in an ongoing, in-depth investigation. Like peeling back an onion, the revelations will make our eyes water …however, these tears will be for the victims.

On November 9, 2011, the university trustees abruptly fired the University President, Graham Spanier, and head football coach Joe Paterno. Why? One could speculate their concerns were predominantly focused on protecting the $70 million and, no doubt, themselves. And, maybe somewhere at the bottom of the priority list of their concerns was protecting the kids who would have been sexually abused in the future and attending to the needs of those who were abused in the past. Maybe.

The complete Penn State sex scandal is just beginning to come to light. My prediction: eventually it will be learned that many people who were (and in some cases still are), part of the power structure of the university system were involved in a cover up of massive proportions. The *dirty little secret* will be discovered and will no longer be *little* and certainly will no longer be a *secret*. The victims will continue to come forward and people at the highest levels in the university system and government will be asked *what they knew and when did they know it*. For example, questions continue about the mysterious disappearance of Ray Gricar, the Center

County, Pennsylvania, District Attorney who was connected to a previous investigation of sex abuse charges against Sandusky. He vanished on April 15, 2005, and the next day his car was found abandoned in an antiques store parking lot and his computer was found in the Susquehanna River with the hard drive missing. (When the FBI later found the hard drive, it was determined it had been removed from Gricar's computer). The Governor of Pennsylvania, who was the state attorney general at the time of the Sandusky investigation, will face demanding questions as well. Powerful big time football kingdoms versus used and "throw away" little kids – stay tuned.

The Public Must Know

The premise of this book is to highlight the need to change how the media and governmental officials deal with child sexual assault cases. Maureen Dowd's column detailing Sandusky having anal intercourse in the shower with a young boy makes us all wince. However, it is essential that the facts about sexual attacks on children be disclosed and we stop hiding the details of these assaults, notwithstanding the wince factor. The public needs to know what these kids go through when sexually assaulted in horrible ways and the tragedies that always follow the child for a lifetime. Sex abuse is not easy to read and learn about, but in order to secure the resources to rescue abused children and to catch sexual predators, the public needs to know exactly what is happening – then the outrage begins followed by the courage to make the badly needed changes.

Once again, just when law enforcement and the public think they've seen it all, another twist in the unique imagination of sex offenders surfaces. Pedophiles are very clever and creative in devising sadistic ways to sexually conquer new victims. Whether it's the stepfather, cop, deacon; or the assistance attorney general, top drug prosecutor – James Cameron; or the award winning kindergarten teacher – Rob Mocarsky; a famous football coach; or the actor and hypnotist – Aaron Patton; or thousands more just like them with their own individual disguises, sex offenders are always in pursuit of unsuspecting victims and mingle among us every day.

They work with us, they worship with us, they take care of and teach our children, they attend to our medical needs and - they protect us.

It's not the purpose of this chapter or this book to make everyone paranoid or to instill in children a constant fear and suspicion of everyone they meet and know. Rather it's the goal of this author that, as caring adults, we become more aware of those who interact with children both on a regular or an infrequent basis. There is a big difference between over protecting and isolating children and allowing them to enjoy a normal life. Common sense tells us to be constantly aware and vigilant of those who play with, supervise or in other ways have influence over children. Talking with children about their daily activities and those who are part of their lives is critically important and is essential to provide a safe and healthy environment for those vulnerable little ones who depend on us to protect them – no matter what it takes.

Just as young Marie tried to send desperate messages for help from anyone who would notice by wearing her clothes inside out while playing outside, different children may be doing whatever they can to send their own urgent pleas for help. Stay alert and look for changes in attitudes, unusual social interactions or other strange and peculiar things children may say or do. Many disguises can work forever, or at least they can be effective for much too long, and that is where our attention and awareness can make a difference.

The **V** shaped design illustrates the vast number of sex offenders who are molesting children, many of whom will never be discovered, compared to the much smaller population that will be caught and successfully prosecuted. When you add the largest group of total offenders to the middle category of those identified, but not prosecuted for whatever reason, it is easy to see the seriousness of this problem and why it requires our utmost attention. We can do our part by being more aware of our children and aggressively engaging the public and our elected officials in conversations demanding greater support for our legal system and law enforcement agencies in their fight to improve the system and to move forward to change *the V to an I.*

CHAPTER 4

THE ADAM WALSH ACT
THE MOTHER OF ALL FEDERAL SEX OFFENDER LAWS

Complex – Costly - Controversial

JOHN WALSH was the long time host of "America's Most Wanted" television show. He and his wife, Reve', had a son, Adam, whose name has now become synonymous with the nationally known and most comprehensive federal law regulating sex offender registration, notification and sentencing.

Things are getting worse

- **800,000 children disappear from their homes every year.**
- **2000 children are abducted every single day**
- **74% are murdered in the first three hours of abduction**
- **1982 - 151,341 missing children**
- **2000 - 876,213 missing children - 468% Increase (f19)**

On July 27, 1981, young Adam Walsh was with his mother, Reve', in the Sears department store at the Hollywood Mall, across from the Police Department in Hollywood, Florida. Reve' left her six-year-old son at the Sears toy department briefly while she looked for a lamp just three aisles away. Adam was abducted after a 17-year-old security guard apparently asked four boys to leave the department store. Adam was believed to be one of the four boys. (f20)

Sixteen days following Adam's disappearance, his head, which had been severed from his body, was found in a drainage canal more than 120 miles from his home. The rest of Adam's body was never found. (f20) The prime suspect in Adam's abduction and murder was a man named Ottis Elward Toole, who lived in Jacksonville, Florida where investigators found a pair of green shorts and a sandal similar to what Adam was wearing the day of his disappearance.

John Walsh was told by Toole's niece that her uncle, lying on his deathbed in prison in 1996, confessed to killing Adam. He abducted Adam from the mall and drove for about an hour to an isolated dirt road where he cut the boy's head off. On December 16, 2008 the Hollywood Police Department officially considered the case closed. (f21)

On the day the police officially closed the Adam Walsh murder case the Police Chief, Chadwick Wagner, acknowledged that several mistakes were made by the department during the investigation and he apologized to the Walsh family. During the investigation it was reported that the police lost critical evidence including the bloody car mat and even Toole's car at one point. This was part of the reason the case was delayed for so long. (f21)

Toole was the worst kind of violent sexual predator who admitted to cannibalism as well as rape, torture and dismembering human bodies - a process he described in chilling detail when being interviewed, especially on camera. Almost bragging, Toole would take great pleasure describing to the media the sexual pleasures he felt when sexually molesting, torturing and even killing his victims. The most devastating realization about Toole's history of violent sexual assaults is the fact that many of his victims were children.

During one filmed interview entitled, "Interview with a Serial Killer Ottis Toole – 1993" distributed by Guilford Ghost, Toole explained how he, "… *would take a baseball bat and shove it down his (a man he wanted to kill) throat until it comes out his ass … or shove a long spike (metal rod) down his throat until it comes out of his ass… then put the body on a barbeque (pit) and roast it – then let people from the street come in and eat it. Then you tell them they just ate a human body! Ha ha, ha."* (f26) As you can see, Toole was one sick son-of-a-bitch!

According to a segment of "America's Most Wanted" television series, Toole, who was a homosexual, met Henry Lee Lucas in 1978 at a Jacksonville soup kitchen and the two of them joined forces as a homosexual crime team, crisscrossing the country from 1978-83 engaging in several killings. One can only imagine the hideous ways they tortured and killed their many victims.

The Adam Walsh Child Protection and Safety Act of 2006 (also known as the Sex Offender Registration and Notification Act or *SORNA, 42 U.S.C. s 16911 et seq.*) was signed into law on July 27, 2006, 25 years to the day after the abduction of Adam. Once again, just like all of the previous well-intended federal laws designed to protect society from child molesters, rapists and murderers, a federal law was written and passed as a result of an individual tragedy. Especially in this case. The father of the murdered boy was a high profile television celebrity whose extraordinary influence with members of Congress no doubt added to the public pressure to pass the new law. The dedication John Walsh and his family demonstrated as they worked to find ways to protect children from pedophiles and to help law enforcement agencies capture sexual predators was admirable and much appreciated. However, the federal law they helped construct, the Adam Walsh Act, is not producing the results desired.

Details of this "mother of all sex offender laws" are forthcoming. But first, I want to tell you about another example of a well known, emotion- driven, public pressure based law that is, this very minute, in the making.

As mentioned earlier, politicians like to be out front on these issues and it is important for them to be seen as caring leaders not only ready but eager to be tough on sex offenders (no argument here). Not a bad instinct as long as due diligence is applied to the process and it does not turn into a "let's see who can be the toughest lawmaker" scenario.

The recent example alluded to above of this get-tough-pass-a-law-and-name-it phenomenon was the case of Casey Anthony, whose trial received national news coverage. Casey was the mother who was accused of killing her 2-year-old daughter, Caylee. Caylee was last seen in 2008 at the Orlando, Florida home she shared with her mother and maternal grandparents. Following Caylee's disappearance, Casey left her parents' home and spent most of the time with friends shopping and partying, telling inquisitive family members and others that Caylee was with the (imaginary) nanny.

As time passed and Anthony could not produce the child, the police became suspicious when they were not contacted about the missing child. Anthony responded with the bizarre story that she was conducting an investigation looking for the nanny who had kidnapped Caylee. Anthony was eventually acquitted of murder resulting in a cry of outrage from the public, most of whom believed that the abundance of circumstantial evidence proved that Anthony did kill her daughter, intentionally or otherwise.

As you could predict, based on the evidence and research presented in this book, individuals in Congress quickly picked up on the public outcry and right on cue, they became "outraged," immediately sensing the emotions of their constituents over Anthony's acquittal. These same lawmakers are now proposing "Caylee's Law" that would allow prosecutors to bring felony charges against parents who do not quickly report missing children. Congress will move to write and pass this law faster than it takes to say $16 trillion debt. Guaranteed the process will be rushed, lacking the appropriate and careful consideration of the unintended consequences, just as what happened when writing the previous laws resulting from individual tragedies and the public outrage that followed them.

As sure as members of Congress want to be reelected and as this chapter is being written in September 2011, there will be a "Caylee's Law" passed sometime in the next several months. In the meantime, similar laws will be written and passed in many individual states, again by state legislators who are being pressured to "do something" and want to appear to be tough and act swiftly by responding to their constituents' demands. These laws will be flawed, rushed, and unfairly impact innocent people and sadly, will do little to protect children from their parents or others who try to assault or even kill them. Imposing a felony charge against a parent for failure to file a report of a missing child by a predetermined, arbitrary date and time, ignores all the extenuating circumstances of each case and the slew of unintended consequences that may result from such a law. Another attempt to make the proverbial square peg fit into the round hole; it won't fit in spite of the well-intentioned pushing and maneuvering.

This is an ill-advised way to write laws and to institute public policy, especially when Congress tries to make one law fit all states and particularly when dealing with highly sensitive issues like sex offender laws. Remember, a law with a kid's name attached to it – Megan's Law, the Jacob Wetterling Act, Jessica's Law, Caylee's Law – most always means bad news. The questionable reasoning for writing these laws would be the same logic used when trying to stop a baby from crying by immediately picking the child up every time it makes a whimper. The same applies to passing sex offender legislation. Immediate rewards are given to the lawmakers for "doing something" even if what is done only complicates the problem at hand.

As noted, lawmakers are quick to absorb public outrage like a paper towel absorbs water on a counter top. Then the table is set for passing what are perceived in the moment as hard-hitting, no tolerance, sex offender laws. In reality these laws are usually ineffective and misdirected - like throwing cotton balls at a wall and expecting them to stick.

In an effort to provide full disclosure, I cosponsored a law in Maine several years ago named after a victim who was killed in a tragic highway accident in 2005. "Tina's Law" was written and passed in 2006 as a result of the death of Tina Turcotte. Her car was struck from behind on the Maine Turnpike by an 18-wheel tractor-trailer driven by a man whose license was under suspension. Common sense assessment would conclude that the driver should not have been allowed to have a license and therefore should not have been driving that day. While continually ignoring the law, this driver had accumulated over 60 traffic violations including more than 20 license suspensions. The purpose of this particular effort was to tighten up the law so that repeat offenders of traffic laws would not be allowed to continue to drive.

Habitual violators had little to fear prior to the passage of this law because it was well established that there were sufficient loopholes available to manipulate the system. The writing of this particular legislation was unique in that I had the advantage of having been Maine's Secretary of State for eight years and was familiar with motor vehicle laws and the accompanying penalties. "Tina's Law" was passed after several months of consideration and involvement by a diverse coalition of interested groups including the Maine Civil Liberties Union (MCLU), law enforcement agencies, defense attorneys, prosecutors and the Secretary of State's office. There was ample time given to study the consequences of each part of the law and the final result was agreed to by all sides. There was no undue pressure in "getting something passed" and the process involved thorough checking and double-checking of every aspect of the legislation as it was being constructed. The end product was a law that did exactly what it was designed to do and there were no significant unintended consequences unfairly impacting innocent people. In fact, the Maine Supreme Court upheld the law when it was challenged a few years later. Unlike most other "named laws" Tina's Law has withstood all challenges and is an exception to my "named laws" rule.

Adam Walsh Act to the Rescue!

These next few pages are designed to give you the needed background to understand the federal law enacted in 2006 that established baseline sex offender registry standards that all states are expected to meet or face the eventual loss of federal grant money if they are not in "substantial compliance." Consider this a personal Adam Walsh Act 101 describing the law in general and how it affects all 50 states. This will be painless and will make the reader, comparatively speaking, an expert regarding this latest and most significant, federal law regulating sex offenders.

The Adam Walsh Act (AWA) fully replaces the Jacob Wetterling sex offender legislation requirements. Although well intended, it creates logistical and financial problems for many states; these states will face a loss of federal funding if they fail to "substantially comply" with the law. Specifically, failure to comply will result in a 10% reduction in federal money that states currently receive from what is known as the Edward Byrne Memorial State and Local Enforcement Justice Assistance Grant Program. The initial deadline for all states to attain "substantial compliance" was July 27, 2009. States were permitted to file a request for an extension for a one-year period. A second one-year extension was also authorized. Many states, including

Maine, requested and received these extensions due to the complexities and cost of implementation of the new law and pending litigation. Only 14 states, nine tribes and the territory of Guam had met the "substantial compliance" requirements as of the final deadline of July 27, 2011, the 30th anniversary of the disappearance of Adam Walsh. Maine did not meet the final deadline and will no doubt be assessed the 10% penalty.

In spite of the Adam Walsh Act, each state has to abide by its own state constitution when writing and passing legislation even when trying to comply with federal laws such as the AWA. When it comes right down to it, state legislatures usually avoid violating their own constitutions even if it means losing federal funds. In Maine, for example, the Supreme Judicial Court has given strong indications that adding new requirements for registrants to meet were found to be more like punishment – *ex post facto* – could very well be a violation of the Maine Constitution. One aspect of the AWA requires that former sex offenders are to be included in the registration requirements. Some of these federal requirements may be in direct conflict with the Maine Constitution.

Ohio was the first state to "substantially comply" with AWA and its Supreme Court has now ruled that some portions of their law are unconstitutional. Ohio must try to find a way to comply with the AWA and still not violate its own constitution. Ohio's version of the Adam Walsh Act has resulted in more than 7000 legal claims, according to the Public Defender's Office. It also has led to years of litigation, two state Supreme Court rulings and separate registry criteria for sex offenders whose crimes occurred before and after the law's enactment.(f22)

States have shown an eagerness to pass sex offender laws; since 2008, 48 states have enacted nearly 350 laws related to residency restrictions, sentencing and monitoring sex offenders, according to the National Conference of State Legislatures (NCSL). "States are very sympathetic to the need to supervise and penalize registered sex offenders. There's no softness on that population. But any time you're going to be collecting and cataloging information on more people more often, that comes at a high cost. The question is whether it's worth it," said Susan Frederick, federal affairs counsel with NCSL.(f22)

Originally the AWA also included a very controversial mandate that required juveniles who are convicted of a sex crime to be placed on the public sex offender registry. The objections to this part of the law were widespread coming from nearly every state. Based on this widespread concern that portion of the law was significantly amended by Congress because they hadn't anticipated the passionate push back from the states on that issue. Therefore, the AWA now requires only juveniles 14 years of age or older at the time of their offense to register if they fit into the most serious tier of offenses. Juveniles who are required to register under the Adam Walsh Act may be eligible for removal from the registry in 25 years if they have a "clean record." Although AWA has changed, some juveniles are still required to register for at least 25 years.

The AWA also established the Sex Offender Sentencing, Monitoring, Apprehending, Registering and Tracking Office ("SMART Office"). One purpose of the SMART office is to support the national implementation of a comprehensive sex offender registry and to determine whether states are in compliance with the law.

There are parts of AWA that make sense conceptually but will still end up costing the states considerable amounts of money. Creating a reliable system that will assess how likely a sex offender will reoffend, and therefore determine their risk level, will be complicated and almost impossible to defend unless the assessment is based solely on the crime committed. Such as system coincides with the AWA as presented at this point. Otherwise, what would be the legal implications? Remember Ottis Toole? He was determined by "experts" to be rehabilitated and had made substantial gains with his sex offender problems so he was released from incarceration. So what does Toole do after being released? He kidnaps Adam Walsh and who knows how many others, and did whatever he did to the child before killing him. Not exactly what the "experts" had predicted.

Alfonso Rodriguez was released from prison in May 2003 after serving 23 years for sexual violence against a woman. He was considered likely to reoffend and yet he still was allowed to go back into the community. Sure enough, a few months after his release, Rodriguez abducted Dru Sjodin, a University of North Dakota student, at a mall parking lot in Grand Forks, North Dakota, on November 22, and raped and murdered her. Rodriguez is now awaiting execution on federal death row. (f23)

A miscalculation such as what happened with Ottis Toole or a broken system that lets someone as dangerous as Rodriguez walk free illustrates the problems with some current laws. It's frustrating to see these dangerous sex offenders, who are likely to reoffend, go free without at least requiring them to wear the monitoring devices that keep close track of the offenders' whereabouts, a strategy that is very expensive.

As mentioned earlier, a practical and defensible way to determine the potential risk of a convicted sex offender is to base that determination on the specific crime(s) committed. That is not a perfect solution, but it's the best option available at the time. Consistency and defensibility need to be the corner stones of this process,

otherwise the infinite number of court appeals and challenges to the process will cause the entire system to crumble under its own weight.

In summary the Adam Walsh Act tier system is categorized in the following way:

Tier I sex offenders convicted of the "least serious" offenses are required to register for <u>15 years</u>, renewing their registration every year. This is a "catch-all" category that includes misdemeanor and felony offenses.

Tier II is for more serious sex offenders who are required to register for <u>25 years</u> renewing their registrations every six months. Those in Tier II have been convicted of the following types of crimes:

- the use of minors in prostitution
- sexual contact with minors (Sexual contact defined in Maine law means: *"Any touching of the genitals or anus, directly or through clothing, …. for the purpose of arousing or gratifying sexual desire…"* Sexual contact in this law involves any type or degree of genital, oral,, or anal penetration or any sexual touching of or contact with a person's body, either directly or through the clothing.)
- the use of a minor in a sexual performance
- the production or distribution of child pornography

Tier III is for the most serious sex offenders who are required to register <u>for life</u> and they must renew their registration every three months. Those assigned to this tier have been convicted of the following types of crimes:

- *sexual acts with another by force or threat [Sexual Act defined in Maine law means: "Any act between 2 persons involving direct physical contact between the genitals on one and the mouth or anus of the other, or direct physical contact between the genitals of one and the genitals of the other." Further definitions of "Sexual Act" include similar language with the use of animals and "instrument or device" manipulations.)*
- engaging in a sex act with another who has been rendered
- unconscious or involuntarily drugged, etc.
- sexual acts with a child under the age of 12
- non-parental kidnapping of a minor (f24)

The "Tier System" concept is an important addition to the structure of the sex offender registries and will definitely be helpful to those who search the registries to find out if there are convicted sex offenders living in their communities.

Plea-bargaining will become more important as prosecutors and defense attorneys build their cases driven by the all-important tiers. Sex offenders who are required to register as a higher tier offender may be more tempted to avoid registration after being released from incarceration and may go underground making their whereabouts difficult to determine. This will result in more law enforcement time and resources of law enforcement agencies to locate the offenders who then may be sent back into the court system at an additional cost. There needs to be a system put in place that can handle the increased number of transactions within the Department of Public Safety. The more information required on each registrant the higher the cost to fund the system.

When all is said and done the Adam Walsh Act will probably never be completely implemented by many states, at least not as it is currently written and intended by Congress. Substantial compliance is not practical because states must first try to abide by their own constitutions, and many have long held beliefs and philosophies about how to implement and administer notification laws. Traditions within each state are strong and many laws have stood the test of time and will be defended, regardless of the resulting loss of federal funds. The Adam Walsh Act was written without first considering the concerns of individual states and therefore could very well become yet another cumbersome, unused, and unappreciated piece of federal legislation. Congress will wake up one day and ask what happened to the "mother of all sex offender laws." They will scratch their heads and wonder what went wrong. Passing a federal law that fits the philosophies of all 50 states is very difficult, especially when the problem at hand is something as sensitive as sex offender legislation.

CHAPTER 5

MAINE STATE POLICE COMPUTER CRIMES UNIT HIDDEN HEROES

"Looking at images of children and toddlers – infants – being sexually molested, raped and seeing the suffering without being able to rescue them immediately, is the toughest part of this job." Lt. Glenn Lang

LIEUTENANT GLENN Lang is the supervisor of the Maine State Police Computer Crime Unit (CCU). "The most important thing we do is find these children that are being used for sexual pleasure," Lang said. These are kids who are filmed and photographed while being raped or made to perform sexual acts with other children, adults and even animals.

The professionals who work daily to find ways to rescue these kids are unique and will tell you that it's bad enough to see older looking children - 14 and 15 year olds - being sexually assaulted, but seeing the most innocent of all – the babies and young children - used in such a manner is the most difficult. When a child is rescued from the ordeals of this torture, exhilaration explodes within the Computer Crimes Unit offices like giant fireworks exploding in the sky. The professional pride and relief experienced by the dedicated investigators who worked hard for many months and, in some cases years, trying to locate and rescue the child is beyond description.

Over the past three years the CCU has found and rescued 26 kids who were used prominently as "sex stars" in the child pornography industry throughout the United States. Lt. Lang says that rescuing 26 kids may not sound like a lot, but it is significant, especially to those 26 children and their families. The child pornography (CP) underworld is so well self-protected and complex that locating an abused child becomes extremely difficult. When a child is found, it's a huge victory, especially knowing what may lie ahead for these kids if they are not saved as quickly as possible is more torture and probably eventual death.

The Computer Crimes Unit (CCU) is a multi-jurisdictional police entity designed primarily to assist other law enforcement agencies and prosecutors with the investigation and prosecution of computer crimes. Computer crimes are those in which a computer is used as an instrument in committing a crime. What started out as primarily a tool for investigating "white collar" crimes soon turned into investigating illegal activities involving the downloading, disseminating and producing of child pornography.

The Internet Crimes Against Children (ICAC) program is composed of Regional Task Forces and Satellites (law enforcement agencies that assist the task forces). ICAC (pronounced eye - cak) focuses on investigations of reported child pornography cases using a number of methods including undercover operations conducted by specially trained police officers. The investigations collect unassailable evidence regarding a suspect's tendency to exploit children. These officers have the training and skill to locate these victims using whatever clues they can extract from the various backgrounds observed in the videos and pictures featuring the child as the central focus. For example, when reviewing images of a child posing in sexually explicit positions in a motel room, investigators will focus first on determining the location of the motel. This sets the stage for directing resources to the most likely geographical area of the country and thus increasing the odds of rescuing the child. In an effort to determine the approximate location of the motel in question, investigators look for the tiniest of clues in the photos or film that might be unique to a particular part of the country.

It could be something as minor as a beer bottle sitting on a table that is a certain type beer brewed or distributed to a particular section of the United States, or it could be other background items reflecting a geographical uniqueness. In one case the bedspread on a motel bed seen in one of the photos appeared unusual, and after extended research, it was discovered that the manufacturing company of that particular bedspread was located in the southeastern part of the United States. The investigators were able to focus their search in a more concentrated area, thus improving their likelihood of success. One clue led to another and before long they found the motel, the captor/offender and most importantly - the little girl. More on that intriguing investigation later in this chapter. Guaranteed the details around this case are captivating.

Along with ICAC, the Computer Crimes Unit works closely with the National Center for Missing and Exploited Children (NCMEC) and the Child Exploitation and Obscenity Section (CEOS) of the United States Attorney's Office in the Department of Justice. The FBI is key to most investigations utilizing their extensive resources to assist state investigations, and they are involved with international rescues when needed.

Peer to Peer Networks - "Hash Values"

The child pornography industry benefits from a global marketplace supported by hundreds of thousands of criminals who use children as sexual commodities. Children are the primary resource and attraction as they are tortured and sexually abused for the purpose of satisfying sexual desires and fetishes of those who will eagerly pay to look at these types of images. The Internet is the vehicle used to transmit and share images of children who have been filmed and photographed in sexually abusive environments. These Internet sites are well guarded by those who control the numerous networks. When individuals go online to share their "pics" (pictures) and "vids" (videos) with each other, they use what is known as "peer-to-peer networks." These networks are designed to facilitate the sharing of electronic files between participating members over the Internet. There are dozens of peer-to-peer clients on the Internet, including the more commonly used *"Kazaa," "Bearshare"* and *"Limewire"*, names the unaware person would not recognize as child pornography sites; however, to those involved, these names are as recognizable as Chevrolet, Cheerios, and McDonald's are to the rest of society.

Becoming a member of a peer-to-peer network requires the installation of a computer program that creates a "sharing folder" on the prospective member's computer into which he or she can insert any electronic files desired. Doing so makes the files available for other members of the network to copy. The member, in turn, gains the ability to copy any electronic files that the other network members have made available on their computers. A single peer-to-peer network may consist of thousands of interconnected computers, and the electronic files available on that network are all stored on the individual members' computers rather than on a central host computer. The avoidance of a host computer makes it much more difficult for law enforcement agencies, resulting in the need to investigate thousands of locations rather than one central computer, which is one of many safeguards the porn industry uses to protect itself.

Because peer-to-peer networks provide an open, convenient and largely unregulated forum for exchanging files, they are very commonly used both for the illegal reproduction of copyrighted or licensed materials (such as music, movies, video games and software) and also for the illegal dissemination of child pornography.

Peer-to-peer networks use "hash values" also known as "sha 1 values" to verify the identity of electronic files that are available for copying. A hash value is a very long series of numbers and letters (such as U6CRWFJYYAKH5PJVFY5QV3N QPXYKA4HG) that is calculated by applying a standard mathematical algorithm to the electronic data that is contained in an electronic file. Only identical files will have the same hash value, and any change to the contents of an electronic file, no matter how slight, will result in a change to that file's hash value. Thus, hash values are commonly referred to as "electronic fingerprints." These networkers are keenly aware of the consequences of being caught, so they go to great technological lengths to avoid being discovered by the authorities.

Peer-to-peer networks rely on Internet protocol (IP) addresses to identify each computer that is sharing electronic files in the network. An IP address is a long string of numbers separated by periods (such as 121.98.332.401), which is assigned to identify each computer that logs onto the Internet and which remains assigned to that computer until it logs off the Internet. IP address assignments are unique in that no two computers logged onto the Internet at the same time will have the same IP address. Ordinarily, when a computer logs off the Internet the IP address that was assigned to that computer may be assigned to another computer logging onto the Internet. IP addresses are assigned in blocks to Internet service providers (such as AOL, Time Warner and Comcast), which in turn assign individual IP addresses to individual subscribers as they log online. Internet service providers usually keep records of the assignment of IP addresses to their individual subscribers. Through resources known to law enforcement to be reliable and available on the Internet, (such as www. checkdomain.com) it is easy to determine which Internet service provider owns a particular IP address or a block of IP addresses and even the general geographic area of the individual subscribers to which a particular IP address has been assigned.

Every computer has its own special identifier and all of the sites that are visited can be revealed one way or another, if needed. Once online everything you do can be tracked. In fact, it's safe to say that there are no secrets in the world of online visitations.

When a member of a peer-to-peer network submits a request for a particular electronic file, like "Madonna," a child pornography site, the network program provides a list of available electronic files that match the request by the same or similar names. The hash value for each available electronic file, and the IP address of each network member currently logged onto the Internet are available for review and examination. The listed electronic files may then be copied from the peer-to-peer network to the requesting member's computer. That's how they get access to the desired child porn videos and pictures.

Law enforcement agents in the United States have discovered that by joining a peer-to-peer network and submitting a request for an electronic file known to contain child pornography, as verified by the file's hash value, they can readily identify the IP addresses of other network members who have attempted to disseminate that particular piece of child pornography by making it available to be copied. Law enforcement agencies in Pennsylvania and Massachusetts host a website, "Data Base 1" that is designed to facilitate this type of investigation. (Their State Police departments have requested that the official name of their database and website not be used, so the database will be referred to as "Data Base 1.") The website is accessible only to law enforcement agents, and it serves as a clearinghouse for information obtained from such investigations conducted by law enforcement agents around the country such as the *Gnutella* peer-to-peer network. (Gnutella is a peer-to-peer computer network on the Internet suspected of being involved in the possession and dissemination of illegal sexually explicit images of children). The website stores the IP addresses that have been identified as offering electronic files known to contain child pornography. The website also provides an automated service that identifies the general geographic area of the subscriber to whom each IP address was assigned, based on the known geographic distribution of blocks of IP addresses assigned by Internet service providers to subscribers. (f25)

It's a constant battle by law enforcement agencies to keep up with the high level technology used by the peer-to-peer networks. The level of sophistication and cunning utilized by the child porn industry is impressive; however, having the ability to identify an individual computer, that's used to view illegal child porn, through its IP address provides a huge advantage for the investigators. When someone goes online to view child porn, the computer is specifically identified as to its geographic location such as the residence where the computer is located.

From that point identifying the user(s) is relatively simple. Once a computer is apprehended, the technology specialists, who are part of the investigative team, can identify which sites have been viewed, stored for future use and/or shared, thus obtaining the evidence necessary for prosecution. Attempts to delete or hide previously visited online sites are usually unsuccessful for several reasons, some of which have been explained here. Those who frequently visit the various child porn sites usually download the pictures and videos saving them for later use, usually for inspiration for masturbation and/or for sharing with people of similar interest.

When a computer has been identified as a peer-to-peer user, sharing known child porn sites, law enforcement agents pick up on the activity and then visit the location of the computer, usually a residence, to initiate an investigation. Standard operation procedure in these cases includes obtaining a search warrant in advance of arriving at the residence in question for the purposes of confiscating the computer (or computers) and onsite searching for videos and pictures downloaded from the peer-to-peer network sites. For some illogical reason the child porn collectors believe that they can store their illegal cache in some secretive place like basements or closets. Some try to even hide their treasure in more creative places like well-hidden "cubby-holes" in sheds, attics, and barns. However, their choice for hiding places must always be relatively accessible to them so that retrieval for personal sexual enjoyment is convenient, meaning the investigators will probably find them. Unfortunately, due to a severe lack of funding to support sufficient numbers of technically trained law enforcement investigators, usually only the high volume online child pornographers are targeted as opposed to going after all users. However, there are occasions when investigations of high volume participants provide leads to other child porn viewers either through association or location.

A national pro-child, anti-crime association known as PROTECT accurately points out that technology has allowed online child porn to proliferate around the world, but the same technology is utilized to apprehend child pornographers and supporters of the industry. PROTECT, on October 6, 2008, stated, "For the first time in history, technology offers the opportunity to detect and stop child sexual abuse on a massive scale. By tracking the distribution of child pornography, law enforcement can go back through the Internet, right to the door of hundreds of thousands of children waiting for rescue."

(PROTECT is a national nonpartisan organization founded on the belief that the first and most sacred obligation of parents and citizens is the protection of children from harm.)

There are many technology tools that law enforcement agencies utilize that will remain confidential so not to impede their constant battle to keep up with the ever elusive and persistent peer-to-peer networks. Even though the technology is available, less than 1% of known child exploitation suspects are investigated due to the lack of resources. Funding is a matter of setting spending priorities and now is the time to make that commitment. If we truly believe that rescuing children from sexual abuse is our top priority, then lawmakers need to come up with the appropriate funding. This is not a time for talking or posturing – we cannot wait any longer and neither can the children.

The "Tara Series" – A Nightmare with a Better Ending

The Maine Computer Crimes Unit played a key role in working with several other law enforcement agencies to identify the location and then to rescue a young girl in what was known as the "Tara Series." ("Tara" is based on the name used to refer to the 9 -11 year-old child who was the "star" of several Internet child porn videos and pictures.) It's common for several states and federal agencies to join forces when looking for children, especially when the sites show increasingly aggressive behavior toward the child featured. For example, concerns escalate when the images of the child "star" start transitioning from the usual nude and semi-nude sexual poses along with oral sex and various forms of intercourse to more aggressive acts that suggest imminent violence towards the child. Filming violence or the threat of violence to a child is one way to keep a certain category of viewer interested so new and more dramatic scenes are incorporated. There are many viewers who achieve sexual arousal by watching a child being subjected to actual or insinuated violent acts, especially if there is a sexual connotation threaded into the scene. Therefore, when this tendency towards violence becomes prevalent, the investigating team raises its level of intensity to rescue the child. Such was the case in the "Tara Series" where scenes of suggested violence against "Tara" were occurring. Specifically, the man who was responsible for the creation and dissemination of the images of "Tara" showed photos of himself standing beside the young girl in a very threatening manner: she was naked and he was holding a large, possibly foot-long wide-blade butcher knife, pressed against her throat just below her chin. The clear message in that scene was that he was going to cut her throat. This told the investigators that "Tara's" life was in more danger than originally thought and they needed to work even harder to rescue her.

December 2007 – the Search for Tara
An Amazing True Life Investigation and Rescue

The FBI describes their special unit, *Innocent Images National Initiative (IINI),* a component of FBI's Cyber Crimes Program, as "an intelligence driven, proactive, multi-agency operation to combat the proliferation of child pornography/child sexual exploitation facilitated by an online computer." The IINI provides centralized coordination and analysis of case information that by its very nature is national and international in scope, requiring unprecedented coordination with state, local, and international governments and among FBI field offices and legal attaches.

Computer telecommunications have become one of the most prevalent techniques used by pedophiles to share illegal photographic images of children and to lure minors into illicit sexual relationships. The Internet has drastically increased the access of the preferential sex offenders to the population they seek to victimize and provides them greater access to a community of people who validate their sexual preferences.(f27)

The FBI states the following mission for the IINI:

"The mission of the IINI is to reduce the vulnerability of children to acts of sexual exploitation and abuse which are facilitated through the use of computers, to identify and rescue child victims, to investigate and prosecute sexual predators who use the Internet and other online services to sexually exploit children for personal or financial gain; and to strengthen the capabilities of federal, state, local, and international law enforcement through training programs and investigative assistance." (f27)

The Richmond (Virginia) FBI Division received a lead from their IINI unit notifying them of "Operation Achilles." Operation Achilles had worked on a news group server that catered to child porn collectors in the country of New Zealand. As a result of investigations by Interpol, Canada and Germany, one of the juvenile child porn victims was identified as possibly being from the Richmond, Virginia area. This geographical section of the country was suspect because one the offenders who had uploaded large quantities of the "Tara Series" was apprehended in the Richmond area. This is another example of apprehending a violator as a result of an associated investigation as discussed earlier.

As the investigation intensified, one of the background items noticed in a scene involving "Tara" was a box of donuts identified as being sold in the Richmond region. As is the case with many clues, this later proved to be faulty information, but it does give an example of how carefully a video scene or photograph is analyzed. It's these types of subtle clues that can be extremely beneficial to an investigation. Also observed in one of the many images was a sample box of Kotex and when the mailing label on the box was digitally enhanced, it was determined to be either 801 Denver, Colorado or 301 Atlanta, Georgia.

It was discovered that there were between 1800 and 2000 known images and or videos in the "Tara Series." One of those videos was entitled "Caitlin in Myrtle Beach" which led investigators to the Myrtle Beach area. The FBI believed they had found bedspreads and draperies similar to those in the Holiday Inn Express in the areas of Myrtle Beach, Little River and Challot. In one of the videos, a TV Guide was found dated May, 2007. Investigation of every little clue is followed through until the clue either proves to be helpful or is not.

As the investigation continued and clues kept surfacing, the FBI determined there were two vehicles involved in some of the filming of "Tara." The child porn industry works diligently to keep the paying viewers' interests by carefully inserting different backgrounds and story themes. In an effort to provide the necessary variety for the viewers, changes are continually made during the filming to include scenes in different yet familiar places like parking lots, abandoned buildings and inside automobiles. One photographing session showed images of Tara sitting in the back seat of a vehicle partially naked in a sexually explicit pose. Identifying the vehicle was a top priority for the investigators. There were two different vehicles used for the photo shoot. One was identified as a 2003 to 2005 Pontiac Aztec, Sunburst Orange, a color that might be registered as gold, red or orange; The other vehicle was white and identified as a late 1980's G series Chevy van with a bare interior.

Careful examination of the photos revealed additional clues. The background in some of the photos showed the surrounding vegetation that, according to the botanists who were contacted during the investigation, can be found in 8 Southeastern states, including Maryland, Virginia, the Carolina's, Georgia, Alabama, Mississippi, Tennessee, Louisiana, Arkansas, and possibly Texas. One of photos showed the vehicle's rear view mirror and, when enhanced, the reflection in the mirror clearly showed several types of trees, bushes and grass that helped confirm the set of vegetation and the correlation to geographic area of the country. The slightest of clues

Enter the Maine Computer Crimes Unit

Maine's involvement in the international investigation of the "Tara Series" could be considered an accident or maybe divine intervention. Lieutenant Glenn Lang, Maine's CCU supervisor, had been attending the National Crimes Against Children Conference for a couple of years and each year the Director of the National Center for the Missing and Exploited Children (NCMEC) referenced earlier would do a presentation where she would chastise the ICAC Units around the country for not doing enough to identify the victims in the various child porn series. The Director would show examples that actually had license plates or registration numbers displayed in the pictures and no one had thought to run them for identification purposes. Lt. Lang said, "To be honest, I felt ashamed that she was absolutely right and said to myself if I ever got a chance to work one of these cases I would."

In the "Tara Series" the FBI was getting desperate to identify the little girl because of the increasing violence shown in the scenes. They took the unusual step of creating a flyer with some redacted pictures of the child asking people to help identify her. The flier was only supposed to be circulated locally, but somehow it was posted online and went nationwide.

When Lt. Lang saw the flyer he recalled, "I thought this was our (Maine's) Units chance." One of the most significant clues noticed in one of the 'Tara' videos was a blue ribbon hanging on the wall, which will be explained in much more detail in this chapter. It just so happens that this blue ribbon had a unique meaning to Lt. Lang – maybe the only investigator involved in the case that would recognize the significance. "My niece had been in 4-H and I thought the ribbon reminded me of the ribbons that they used to give at the animal shows. (My associate) and I worked the angle and she found the ribbon was an "It's a Boy" ribbon. We were amazed at how fast the identification took place and it just fueled the fire for us to go after more clues in the pictures and the videos."

Maybe it was just luck, more likely sheer determination and dedication that prompted Maine's Computer Crimes Unit to get involved with the "Tara Series." Certainly recognizing the potential of the blue ribbon clue was key to rescuing the little girl. Thank God for Maine's involvement, whether it was by accident or divine intervention.

On May 23, 2008, the Maine CCU received the "Tara" flyer from the FBI, as did most other states, requesting assistance in locating the suspect or victim in this case. The flyer showed headshots of "Tara," some depicting a sexual pose, but others showing a face with eyes revealing a little soul that was almost dead. The Maine CCU did the initial analysis of the pictures in the flyer and identified the aforementioned large blue ribbon hanging on the wall in the background of the photograph. The particular blue ribbon with the words, "It's a Boy", is used to celebrate and congratulate the birth of a new baby boy. Luckily, the ribbon turned out to be unique. The next day, May 24, members in the CCU were assigned to track down the manufacturer and distributor of the ribbon. Three days later the unit received a full resolution picture of the blue ribbon from the FBI for comparison purposes. On May 28, the CCU discovered that the ribbon was manufactured by "Balloons, Inc." a company that produces two types of ribbons. One type of ribbon is customized with a hospital's name imprinted on it. The other type is plain without wording as seen in the FBI flyer. The majority of the ribbons that are sold have a hospital's name imprinted on them, which made this particular ribbon unique in that it was *not* customized.

The Computer Crimes Unit was supplied a customer list of the vendors across the United States that purchased the non-customized ribbons. The list included hospital gift shops and floral shops. Balloons, Inc. does not sell to the general public or over the Internet; therefore, following the trail of clues was a little more condensed. The investigation revealed that 17 states purchased the ribbon: West Virginia, Virginia, Texas, Tennessee, North and South Carolina, Ohio, Mississippi, Missouri, Michigan, Maine, Louisiana, Kentucky, Georgia, Florida, Arkansas and Alabama. It was learned that the vast majority of the ribbons went to the Southeastern part of the United States.

There was something that made this particular ribbon unique in another way. The ribbon was composed of two bows, a larger one on the top of the ribbon and a smaller one at the bottom of the ribbon. In between the two bows was the previously mentioned "It's a Boy" wording. What made this ribbon so different were the two additional decorative items that were attached to the lower bow. These types of non-customized ribbons were sent to Franklin Memorial Hospital in Farmington, Maine. The CCU contacted the hospital gift shop manager and was told the gift shop was operated by volunteers and there were no records kept of their inventory. It was confirmed that the ribbons were sold at the gift shop, but the manager was unsure who purchased them in the past, when they last ordered the ribbon and/or when the last ribbon was sold. Furthermore, the manager stated that many people who volunteer at the gift shop only work there for 3-4 hours a couple times a week. This was a valuable clue that seemed to hit a stonewall but could be used later in the investigation.

On May 30, 2008, the CCU began the off-line searches of the various Departments of Motor Vehicles looking for all 2003 – 2005 orange Pontiac Aztecs in the 17 identified states where the ribbon had been sold. On June 4, the CCU requested assistance from the ICAC (Internet Crimes Against Children) units in the Southeastern United States. They requested these units to check their Motor Vehicle Bureaus for the Sunburst Orange Aztec's. They also requested that ICAC send their investigators to track down their registered owners and conduct interviews. As the off-line searches with the various DMV's produced results, that information was passed on to the corresponding ICAC units. In an effort to leave no stone unturned, the Maine CCU assigned new State Police recruits to contact the registered owners of the vehicles to determine which of them had been contacted and interviewed and which still needed to be contacted.

On June 5, the Wyoming ICAC Peer-to-Peer database was searched for "Tara Series" files. It was discovered that many of the "Tara" videos started spreading from the Southeastern part of the United States. The CCU continued to download and examine "Tara" videos from this network. It was helpful that a number of complete videos involving "Tara" were successfully downloaded and examined. The retrieved "Tara" movies and images were processed to look for any corresponding metadata (data about data) – none was found in the videos. In some of the raw (unchanged or reproduced) data they were able to determine the camera used by the suspect was a Fuji, model Finepic 2300. Cameras have their own "fingerprints" too.

The CCU contacted the Maine Department of Education to establish a protocol to allow a limited distribution of a picture of "Tara" to Maine teachers. A flyer was sent to these teachers, including a clothed picture of "Tara" standing next to a bed. This initiative created several leads, but none of them led to the identification or location of the little girl.

Remember the box of Kotex observed in one of the Tara films? The FBI learned that the distributor of the Kotex samples was a company called Start Sampling. They obtained the database of the distributors and found that six million samples were sent out starting in December 2007 and ending in March of 2008. One of the sample boxes was seen in a photograph with a partial zip code that could have been from the Southeastern United States. The Kotex samples were only sent to households where females resided. In addition, a box of home hair permanent solutions was seen in some of the still images. It was assumed that there was a female living at the residence of the perpetrator.

The Computer Crimes Unit continued to examine many of the videos and images. In the videos, Mardi Gras masks were worn by both the victim and assailant. After examining further videos and images, it was apparent that the man always disguised his face, concealed it or positioned the camera in such a way that the viewer would not see his head. In addition, it was also noted in one of the videos that the victim, "Tara," had a strong southern accent.

As a result of investigations over the peer-to-peer network, the CCU asked the Washington State ICAC to conduct a search warrant in the home of a child pornography collector who had many of the "Tara" videos on his computer. The search resulted in the seizure of many child pornography pictures and videos and the identification of a collector of child pornography. The suspect, however, did not appear to have a connection to the "Tara Series" producer/disseminator. This was a case where law enforcement ended up apprehending an active child porn network member as a side benefit while working on the primary rescue effort.

Bedspreads and Draperies

The CCU contacted random hotel rooms in Augusta, Maine to inquire as to the manufacturers of their bedspreads, curtains, and/or paintings. Working from pictures of the bedspreads and draperies observed in the motel room scenes, efforts were made to identify the origination of these items. Names of various manufacturers were identified and one company, out of Boston, was reported multiple times, Group 1 Partners, Inc. CCU followed up with the president of this company who reported that they do business with many hotels in the Maine area and would be willing to view the redacted image of the hotel room to see if they could visually identify where the bedding, drapes, etc. originated from. It was learned that various vendors identified the drapery fabric, "Hailey on Oz," a reference to the type of pattern on the drapery, made by Richloom Fabrics. However, it was impossible to identify the base cloth that was used in the pattern and therefore, difficult to identify with certainty, the drapery. After viewing the image of the bedding, it was determined that the cloth used in the bedding was named *Path OZ* and had been sold to a company called Fabtex out of Orange, California.

The "Inspired Hillsides" Painting

The CCU determined the painting that was displayed in the hotel room where "Tara" was abused was manufactured by Winn Devon and entitled, "Inspired Hillsides 1" by artist, U. Dell. The investigative team followed up with Encore Art Group/Winn Devon and spoke to a representative out of Canada. The U.S. Attorney's office supplied a subpoena to attain the records of all the customers that purchased this particular picture. It was suggested that the Unit should focus on the wholesale supply companies and the retailers. Various wholesale supply companies located in the Southeastern area of the country were contacted and the CCU began excluding those who reported that they do not sell to hotel chains.

Maybe - Just Maybe

Fabtex reported that their company did purchase the Path OZ bedding on December 1,2006, which was sold to Best Western International, Inc. The U.S. Attorney's office submitted a subpoena for records from the Best Western and was able to learn the purchase order number for this bedding: 555 yards of Paths OZ bedding, color soapstone. The results of the subpoena indicated that the hotel was the Lookout Lodge, out of Phoenix, Arizona. The manager of Lookout Lodge was contacted and confirmed the purchase of the bedding. After reviewing the redacted image of the hotel room, it was reported that the bedding was definitely a match, but the hotel room was definitely <u>NOT</u> a match.

The investigators discovered that Richloom Fabrics sold fabrics to other companies such as Merlin Manufacturing. They, in turn, were contacted and submitted a list of all the properties to whom this Path OZ bedding and Hailey curtains had been sold. Each of the hotels/motels was researched online and they identified two hotel properties that contained the bedding, curtains and the portrait all seen in the hotel room where "Tara" had been abused. The Jamison Inn in Carrollton, Georgia was contacted and after emailing the manager a redacted picture of the "Tara" hotel room it was confirmed that – *finally* – *this was their hotel room!*

Administrative personnel at the Jamison Inn reported that their customer vehicle records were stored in their attic and not computerized. They were told that a subpoena would be served on them for those records, for the approximate date of July 7, 2007. It would be for any customers who had a 2003 – 2005 orange Pontiac Aztec. The Jamison Inn contacted the CCU and reported that they had checked their records and there had been no one with an Aztec who checked in during that weekend. The CCU notified the hotel about the possibility of a *white van* being used by the suspect. As a result, the hotel reported that they had a driver's license picture of a gentleman who drove a *white van* signing into the hotel on July 21, 2007. Questions were asked about payment and check in time. The hotel reported that this male paid in cash, looked, "like someone that would do something like that," and checked in on the July 21 date during the morning hours. There was no check out time and it was assumed that he just left without properly checking out at the front desk.

Finally -Tara Rescued!

After investigators reviewed the information from the hotel files, the name of **James Bartholomew Huskey**, DOB 9/13/1969, was obtained from the driver's license. The license was enlarged and faxed to the Maine CCU. After viewing and comparing the fax copy of the driver's image in the FBI flyer, the FBI was contacted. Based on the information available, the FBI obtained a search warrant and conducted a search of the home of Mr. Husky in LaFayette, Georgia. Georgia's Bureau of Criminal Investigation assisted with the search. As a result of the home search and interview with Mr. Husky, he was arrested.(f28)

James Huskey admitted to abusing the girl and sending the images online. In fact, the girl confirmed that on the very day he was arrested in June 2008, he had violently sexually assaulted her.(f29) He had two children who were taken into protective custody by Georgia authorities. The victim, "Tara", was identified and she confirmed the assaults and filming. The immediate risk and nightmare for "Tara" was over, but her life would never be the same and fortunately, neither would the life of James Huskey.

Huskey pleaded guilty to the charges on November 25, 2008. He was sentenced on March 5, 2009 to serve 70 years in prison on charges of producing, distributing, and receiving child pornography. If he is still alive, following his prison term, he will be required to have supervised release for the rest of his life.

The United States Attorney of Georgia, David E. Nahmias said, "This case ranks among the worst cases of child sexual exploitation we have ever seen. This defendant violently abused a very young girl for several years for his own and others' sexual pleasure. He has caused irreparable harm to his victim's emotional and psychological development. As we know from experts, child sexual abuse can lead to many problems for the victims for their entire lives. In this case, the victim will also have to cope with the knowledge that Huskey used her to produce one of the most notorious series of child pornography traded online worldwide. It is unfortunately common to see the same images of sexually exploited children for years or even decades. This case is a tribute to the cooperative work of law enforcement around the world, who worked diligently together to find this child and arrest her abuser. The defendant deserves every day of the 70-year prison sentence he received."

The "Tara Series" ended up being a huge success. The child was rescued; a violent sexual predator was caught and sentenced to a long, if not life, term in prison where these types of criminals sometimes have to face a different court of judges. The most significant downside in this case is the life long issues that "Tara" faces, as do all children who lived through these traumatic ordeals.

The Maine Computer Crimes Unit can take great pride in the work that they do, but they can be especially proud of the key role they played in identifying and locating a violent predator and rescuing the little girl in the "Tara Series." Without their diligence and determination there is a question whether this case would have been solved – at least in time to save a young life.

As gratifying as the "Tara" investigation was to all involved, the Maine Computer Crimes Unit never rests and there is always another child to rescue and additional predators to capture and prosecute. International investigations usually get a moderate amount of, albeit brief, media attention. Those cases that remain isolated within individual states get much less attention. And, regardless of how heinous the sexual attacks, the best that can be hoped for is one-day media attention with limited follow up coverage of any convictions. This lack of details to the public only adds to the sanitizing of these horrific crimes against children. Uncovering these sexual assaults is a step towards public support for the ICAC's around the country, thus improving the funding and resources needed to rescue the children who have little time to wait.

Devastating Reality

The most shocking details of sexual molestation are those where the victims are infants – some as young as two months old. You will read about such a case in the next several pages. The images described are harsh, and you will not be shielded from the nearly crippling facts of the case. The details will jerk you out of your comfort zone like a bloody screech waking you in the middle of the night. Having to acknowledge that these kinds of predators not only exist, but could be living next door will send chills down your spine and at least for a while – nothing will be able to make you forget or make it stop.

"Worst Case I've Ever Seen in Maine"

Lt. Lang described what he called the worst case of child molestation that he has ever seen in Maine. For those working at the Computer Crimes Unit, these are the types of investigations that eat at the gut, especially when examining the actual images of the assaults. How does one prepare and then deal with the worst kind of sexual attack on a defenseless baby? This next true story is an example of why parents should never put their infants in the control of anyone who is not a well known family member unless that person is absolutely trusted beyond question – trusted with someone more precious than anything else in life.

Sanford, Maine, is a blue-collar community located in York County with a population of approximately 11,000 citizens and an average median household income of $38,000.

In April 2005, Tina and Stephan Bickart appeared as the normal married couple residing in their apartment in the community. However, they were anything but normal. They were sexual predators who had fantasies about engaging in explicit sex acts with children and babies. On this night in April the Bickarts would live out some of their sexual fantasies as together they sexually molested a helpless two-year old baby girl in what can only be described as the one the sickest and most despicable sexual assaults one could imagine.

According to court records, on that night when Stephan returned home from work they both smoked marijuana and cocaine and drank alcohol. Tina told her husband that she had a gift or present for him later on. Later Tina told Stephen to go into the bedroom and "get ready," which he did - he got undressed. Tina then entered the room naked, carrying a two-year old girl who lived next door and whom Tina had offered to babysit and keep overnight. There in the bedroom was Tina, holding the baby – both naked -- and Stephan standing there naked as well waiting for his "present."

Tina put the baby on the bed (or possibly a chair) and inserted her finger into the baby's vagina. She had Stephen join them on the bed and Tina then assisted Stephen as he inserted his penis into the rectum of the baby resulting in anal intercourse. As these sexual assaults on the baby continued into the evening, they both took photographs with their digital camera, thus providing pictorial memories for them and later to their despair …evidence for the police.(f30)

There is No Honor Among Thieves

Weeks later, on June 11, 2005, Sanford Police Officer Richard Bucklin went to the Bickart's apartment because Tina had filed a complaint against Stephen, after they had separated, because he had been calling and harassing her all day. Officer Bucklin told Stephen to stop calling Tina and to let the divorce process deal with their problems. Revenge has two sharp edges and can cut both ways, and it did in this case. Approximately an hour after Officer Bucklin's visit to the apartment, Stephen went to the Sanford Police Station and told Bucklin that Tina had threatened to file a charge against him for sexually abusing her 12-year-old daughter. Stephen denied the accusation, but said that he had something else to tell the officer and handed Bucklin a computer "floppy" disk. Stephen said that he had found the disk in his belongings when packing to leave the apartment when they separated. Stephen also said the disk contained two pictures: one with Tina's finger penetrating (the vagina) of the baby, and one of the baby lying with her head on a pillow crying. After waiving his Miranda rights, Stephen admitted that he was involved in the sexual abuse shown on the disk and gave his account of what happened that night, including the specific involvement by Tina.

Stephan was arrested and pled guilty to attempted gross sexual assault and two lesser crimes for his part in the abuse. As a result, he was sentenced to six and a half years in prison and six and a half years of probation. (f30) Stephen Bickart is listed on Maine's Sex Offender Registry and is one of the examples of a violent sexual predator who *should* be on the sex offender registry and upon release from prison monitored closely by law enforcement authorities for the remainder of his life – a provision known as "supervised released." In fact, it could be argued that Stephen's crime was so heinous that even supervised release may not be sufficient unless maximum supervision is instituted in his case. Perhaps a better option for Stephen Bickart would be to keep him incarcerated for a longer period of time. Supervised release is a relatively new option for the sentencing courts and can only be used if probation in not part of the sentence. Supervised release will be discussed in detail in an upcoming chapter.

Tina Bickart was also arrested as a result of the evidence obtained from the floppy disk pictures and charged with six offenses for her involvement in the sexual assault on the baby. (1) Unlawful sexual contact; (2) Gross sexual assault; (3) Endangering the welfare of a child; (4) Sexual exploitation of a minor; (5) Possession of sexually explicit materials; and (6) Conspiracy to commit gross sexual assault. She went to trial and the jury found her guilty on all counts. Tina Bickart was sentenced to 18 years in prison, with all but 15 years suspended and when released she must be on probation for five years. Sexually molesting a two-year-old baby with digital penetration and assisting her husband to rape the baby and only receives a 15-year sentence? Does that seem just? Fair? Fitting? And, why did Stephen get only 6 ½ years? Anal intercourse with a 24-month-old baby - 6 ½ years?

"On the Other Hand"

The Computer Crimes Unit once again played a key role in the investigation and conviction of both individuals, especially Tina. Stephan pled guilty knowing the evidence against him was overwhelming and presented an opportunity to work a deal that would reduce his prison sentence and at the same time get back at Tina as well. Tina's conviction, on the other hand, could have been a much more difficult if it wasn't for the relatively new field of forensic investigation - using "palm creases" from the palm of the human hand to identify a person similar to how fingerprints are commonly used. When Tina was inserting her finger into the victim, her palm was facing up and therefore, the picture on the disk shows a hand – palm up. Lt. Lang and a detective from the CCU went to the Sanford Police Department to interview Tina shortly after her arrest. After she reluctantly agreed and with the urging of the District Attorney, photos were taken of her hand placed in the same position as shown in the pictures from the disk. The images were printed and compared by experts and the distinguishing "palm creases" were a match in both sets of photos. Tina appealed this technique of palm identification and it went all the way to the Maine Supreme Court that ruled on January 20, 2009 in favor of the lower court's decision to allow palm creases to be used as credible evidence for the purposes of identification.

Tina Bickart, born July 20, 1973, is currently serving her sentence at the Maine Correctional Center in Windham, Maine, the prison facility for females in Maine who have been sentenced for more than nine months. Tina will not be eligible for release until at least April 16, 2020, and then will be on probation for five years. She will be nearly 47 years old, a relatively young age, at the time of release, and only 52 when she completes probation.

Tina, like Stephen, will be listed on Maine's Sex Offender Registry, and they are living examples of the importance of having a registry that is reliable and usable, both for the public and for law enforcement agencies. The registry needs to be redesigned to incorporate a tier system that clearly distinguishes the most serious offenders, like these two, from those who pose less of a risk. The registry needs to speak in plain language with appropriate details so that the average person will be able to distinguish between those who rape babies and someone who was having consensual sex with his under age high school girlfriend. Mixing them together, as we do now, is confusing and does not serve the public well. One should not have to be a lawyer to determine the offenses associated with each registrant.

The Computer Crimes Unit provides a tremendous service to Maine and the nation and deserves support and appreciation. These professionals do their job behind the scenes every day as they work to rescue children and put the bad men and women in prison. Regrettably, the CCU has not received the appropriate support of the various administrations of the Department of Public Safety over the years. However, the CCU has somehow been able to maintain a basic budget by scrambling for federal grants and gathering crumbs from the state budget wherever possible. If legislators and policy makers are serious about rescuing sexually abused children and taking violent sexual predators off the streets, then appropriate support is required now. There is no excuse for treating this CCU like, as they say, "a rented mule." To the men and women in the Maine Computer Crimes Unit who have devoted their lives to quietly rescuing children – and who have had to fight for every scrap of funding just to keep the doors open -- thank you! The little girl in Sanford thanks you. "Tara" says thank you. The parents of those kindergarten children in Jackman, Maine say thank you. The 26 children the CCU helped rescue from all over the country say thank you.

In spite of the many obstacles the CCU has had to overcome just to maintain their existence, these unique law enforcement officers have remained professional and have stayed focused on the important job of saving kids. The message is heartfelt and direct: Maine needs you - the nation needs you – families in their most frightened and desperate times need you – and most of all the children and infants need you. "Non illegitimi carborundum!" (Don't let the bastards get you down!)

The very core of this book screams out for the need for change. Change in the approach of how we watch over the children and our awareness of potential danger to our kids. Change in our priorities in funding, supporting, and structuring the public safety system, in particular the Maine Computer Crimes Unit. Change in the design of our sex offender registry. Change in the laws that let serious sex offenders go free when we know damn well some of the most dangerous among them will likely reoffend, e.g. Ottis Toole (Adam Walsh); Jesse Timmendequos (Megan Kanka), and too many more. In reality, we're not even treading water – not even holding our own against the evilness -- because the public does not really understand the severity of the assaults on our children. Most people have been protected from the gruesome details and the quantity of the suffering for so long that now we face a more significant problem that can only be described as a prolific and silent carnage. Communities are losing this battle, and the shame of it all is that they may not recognize their defeat until it's too late - at least for too many kids.

CHAPTER 6

THE PLAN
HOW TO FIX A BROKEN SYSTEM

IT'S CUMBERSOME, difficult to understand, a magnet for litigation, unfair, and, depending on the luck of the draw, could be downright fatal. This is not a description of a bad marriage, but rather it is a perfect description of Maine's Sex Offender Registry. Unfortunately, Maine is not unique in having a somewhat dysfunctional sex offender registry; it's a problem facing most states. We have seen the over reactive, knee jerk nature that too often controls the structure of our registries leaving a tangled morass of unintended consequences with each attempt to make improvements. There is plenty of blame to go around, such as, Congress continually passing new laws and state legislatures doing the same usually based on high profile tragedies. The results: a mess.

The Adam Walsh Act, the newest federal law, is flying in the face of various state constitutions, thus making it difficult, if not impossible, for states to substantially comply. Every state legislative session brings with it a variety of new sex offender laws usually presented by legislators with good intentions who have little or no background in this complex area. As a result, these efforts most often end up just adding to the mass of incoherent contradictions – like a cow on ice with its feet going in every direction, then falling in a heap, spread eagle and dysfunctional.

Fixing the sex offender registry requires focusing on the categories based on the potential risk a released offender poses to society. The Adam Walsh Act creates three categories or "tiers" as previously outlined and quickly reviewed here.

Tier I: Offenders who are considered to be of the least risk and include those who committed misdemeanors and low level felonies. This is the catch-all level that requires registrants to be on the list for 15 years.

Tier II: Offenders who were involved with minors in prostitution, having had sexual contact with minors, sexual performance with minors, or child pornography. These registrants must be on the list for 25 years.

Tier III: Offenders who were involved with sex acts by force or threat, had sexual contact with someone unconscious, sex with a child under age 12, or non- parental kidnapping. These registrants must remain on the list for life and are required to reregister every three months.

Also, required under the Adam Walsh Act, all tiers on the registry must display the names, addresses and photos of the registrants for the public to view on the world wide Internet.

This particular Tier system is not practical in many ways. First, the lowest risk offenders, those who pose little risk to society, must stay on the registry, that means on the Internet, for 15 years. This does not make sense. It not only ignores the low risk factor, but it unnecessarily adds people to the already cumbersome registry. Add that to the problem, as mentioned earlier, of the lack of clarity and distinction of the severity of the many offenses listed and the confusion only mounts. One only needs to visit the sex offender registry website to realize that, in most cases, distinguishing between the potentially dangerous offenders based on their listed convictions and those no-risk offenders with their accompanying list of offenses is difficult because of the "insider" legal terms used to describe the crimes committed.

Step one - A Sex Offender Registry that Makes Sense

The first component of the Plan creates a more functional design of the sex offender registry by restricting public information to law enforcement agencies and those who make a direct request to the department of pubic safety for specific information about a registrant. There will not be a tier associated with this group of offenders; however, there should be recognition of the need to create a category of low risk offenders providing the courts with another tool in sentencing. For example, a permanently bed ridden elderly nursing home patient should not be required to appear on the Internet or reregister with the state every 6 months or yearly. There are other instances suggesting a commonsense application would be appropriate. Occasionally teens might engage in sophomoric pranks such as taking nude or nearly nude photos of themselves or others with no deviant purpose. This reference does not include similar photos of victims under the age of 12, which is a Class C crime and should remain as such. The concept should be explored as part of the suggested ways to improve the sex offender registry.

The first level of potential risk offenders would be referred to as *Tier A* and would be required to remain on the sex offender registry for 10 years and must verify their information annually. As with all tier placements, any subsequent sex offender convictions would result in placement on a more restrictive tier.

The two remaining proposed Tiers B and C continue to reflect placements based on the more serious crimes. Under this Plan Tier B offenders must stay on the registry for 25 years and Tier C lifetime assignment. Specific examples of crimes with corresponding Tier placements are described as follows:

Tier A: Remain on the registry for 10 years and verify information annually. This tier contains all of the low level felonies and other misdemeanors currently requiring registration.

Tier B: Remain on the registry for 25 years and verify information every six months. Offenses include any sexual contact with minors, sexual performance with minors and possession of child pornography. This category is similar to the proposed Adam Walsh Act Tier requiring 25-year registration on the registry.

Tier C: Remain on the registry for Life – verify information every three months. Registrants are sexually violent offenders who are considered the most dangerous and likely to reoffend and those who are repeat offenders. Examples include molesting children under the age of 14 and having sex with a minor under the age of 14.

These changes in the Maine's Sex Offender Registry could be helpful as Maine attempts to be in "substantial compliance" with the requirements of the Adam Walsh Act. However, substantial compliance should be a secondary goal to the first priority of doing what best protects the citizens of Maine and adheres to the guidelines of the constitution.

Step Two – What Does that Really Mean?

The next step in the new design of the sex offender registry is the implementation of a dramatic change in the descriptions of the offenders' convictions. This proposal requires the registrants' personal information to include an explanation of the offenses stated in lay terminology. Currently, legalese is the standard terminology used to explain the offenses of each registrant. This new component would make the sex offender registry a more practical tool for the average citizen to use and would provide a more realistic understanding of the profile of the registrant.

For example, common terminology previously used to describe a specific conviction is "gross sexual misconduct," a term that can be interpreted in a variety of ways by most people. The following is a specific example of what the Maine Sex Offender Registry makes available to the viewer on its website as opposed to the actual details of the crimes committed. The differences between the two are astounding and eye opening, thus reinforcing the need for clarity. The Criminal Justice and Public Safety Committee in the Maine Legislature has committed to addressing this issue and deserve credit for their willingness to make this badly needed change in Maine's Sex Offender Registry.

In May, 1997 the Maine Supreme Judicial Court issued their ruling regarding an appeal to the court by Milton Thompson in the case: *State of Maine V. Milton Thompson*. (f36) Milton Thompson was found guilty by jury of two counts of gross sexual misconduct (Class A crime), two counts of gross sexual assault (Class B), and one count of unlawful sexual contact (Class C). (Generally speaking Classes A – C crimes are what were formerly known as felonies and Classes D & E were the former misdemeanors, with a couple of exceptions, in Maine.) Thompson appealed his convictions based on several contentions; however the high court ruled that with the exception of one of the five counts, the lower court's actions were appropriate and thus were sustained. The only conviction that was vacated was count 3 because of insufficient evidence that the offense occurred within the six-year statute of limitations. The court gave Thompson an "acquittal" on that one count as they confirmed the convictions on all of the other counts.

Online in the Maine Sex Offender Registry under "Milton Thompson," the following information is provided: Name, address (both mailing and residence), date address last verified, and a photo of Thompson. This is understandable and helpful information. However, when seeking to find the exact crimes Thompson committed things get a little less clear. The information shows that one of his offenses was "unlawful sexual contact." What does that mean to the average citizen? Probably many different images come to mind. In the section on the registry "Statutory Description" it says, *"Intentionally subjecting another person to any sexual contact and the other person has not expressly or impliedly acquiesced in the sexual contact."* It goes on to say that Thompson was convicted in Superior Court in Portland, Maine with a conviction date of 11/29/1993. (f37)

Thompson's other convictions are detailed in the same manner and listed as: Gross sexual assault, gross sexual misconduct, and unlawful sexual contact. The statutory description given for "gross sexual assault" is, *"engaging in a sexual act with another person and the other person has not in fact attained the age of 18 years and the actor is a parent, stepparent, foster parent, guardian or other similar person responsible for the long-term and care and welfare of that other person."* Such a description does provide a little more clarity; however, it still does not explain the specific severity of Thompson's crime. Engaging in a sexual act with someone under the age of 18 does not indicate what really happened and that Thompson sexually violated his two young daughters in several hideous ways.

Therefore, we have the explanations of the convictions that are listed on the sex offender registry designed to provide helpful and useful information to the public regarding Milton Thompson and the crimes he committed. However, in reality Thompson's crimes were more heinous than the description reveals. If the registry is going to be credible and reliable, it must provide an understandable portrayal of the crimes committed. If the sex offender registry is going to be the "go-to" reference site, then it needs to be practical document. Let's take a look at Thompson's crimes – what

81

he really did. Again, in the written decision from the Supreme Court, the following details of Thompson's convictions are stated as follows:

"In May 1994 complaints were filed against Thompson in the District Court (Bridgton), alleging gross sexual misconduct with his older daughter on or about May 4, 1988, to June 30, 1988, and unlawful sexual contact on or about May 4, 1988. In November 1994 Thompson was indicted by a Cumberland grand jury on charges of gross sexual misconduct (Counts I and III), (statutory reference), gross sexual assault (Counts IV and V), (statutory reference), and unlawful sexual contact (Count II), (statutory reference). Count I named his older daughter as the victim and alleged sexual misconduct with her "on or about the time period between and including the Fourth day of May and the Thirtieth day of June 1988"; Count II alleged that Thompson subjected his older daughter to sexual contact "on or about the Fourth day of May 1988"; Count III alleged gross sexual misconduct with his older daughter during a period from on or about November 14, 1988, to January 10, 1989; Counts IV and V alleged gross sexual assault against Thompson's younger daughter. (1) All of the counts alleged that the criminal activity occurred in Naples.

At the Trial the older daughter testified that the family moved to her grandmother's house in Naples when she was 12, at the end of her sixth-grade year. Thompson forced her to engage in anal intercourse there in May and June in 1988, three or four times a week, in the middle of the day. The older daughter also stated that between May 1988 and January 1989, prior to her fourteenth birthday, (2) Thompson touched her vagina with his hand at night in her bedroom in the Naples house. The older daughter also admitted that she originally told one of the police detectives that the abuse happened in the spring of 1988, that it was "the last" time she remembered her father touching her, and that she considered "spring" to be "March, April.

Both daughters testified as to "prior bad acts" committed by Thompson.

The older daughter testified that when she was 12 years old and living with her family in Norway, she asked her father to buy one of her favorite sandwiches and that he said he would if she would go out in the woods with him and sit on his face. She refused. A few days later she was at home sleeping in the room she shared with one of her sisters. She awoke to find the radio in the room covered with a pillow and her father sitting at the end of her bed, removing her covers and her underwear, putting his face between her legs, and licking her vagina. The younger daughter testified that she remembered "things happened with her dad" starting when she was nine years old and they lived in Naples, and that she had more detailed memories of things that happened to her later, when they lived in South Paris, Norway, and Mechanic Falls (by which time she was 15 or 16), including Thompson touching and licking her vagina.

The older daughter also testified on cross-examination about her differences with her parents over money. The State then asked about her father's unsolicited offers of money in exchange for sexual favors. The court allowed this testimony over Thompson's objections because he had raised the specter during cross-examination of the older daughter "that the charges are being fabricated by a vindictive daughter who is not getting adequate support for her post-secondary education." (f36)

Milton Thompson was convicted on all counts in Superior Court. However, as stated earlier, he appealed his convictions to the Maine Supreme Judicial Court.

The Court's decision, in part, is as follows:

> *"Thompson appeals from his jury convictions on Counts I and III for gross sexual misconduct and on Count II for unlawful sexual contact, claiming that the evidence was insufficient to prove beyond a reasonable doubt that the offenses alleged occurred within the six-year statute of limitations. .....A prosecution for a Class A, B or C crime must be commenced within six years after it is committed."* (f36)

The Court and the State agreed that there was insufficient evidence to convict Thompson of count III, gross sexual misconduct, because of the possible timing of the offense in relation to the statute of limitations. That was the only count where an acquittal was granted.

Forcing anal intercourse with his daughter! Licking his daughter's vagina! Trying to persuade her to sit on his face! Those perversions give a much different picture of the offender than the vague descriptions provided on the registry. If the purpose of the registry is to help the public understand in real terms the offenses committed by each registrant so that an appropriate degree of concern can be attributed to those on the registry, then writing the descriptions so that most people can comprehend them is essential. Obviously, this case demonstrates that clear and recognizable language must be an integral part of the sex offender registry that can be achieved by implementing a summary, in lay terms, of each offense. Unfortunately, this example illustrates the norm as opposed to an anomaly. There are many ways to approach a written summary of the convictions and this should be an easy task to accomplish. Knowing the specifics of Thompson's convictions, compared to the information available, leaves the average person begging for a change, a change that will make the registry more functional by using understandable language and thus, becoming more credible.

Step Three - Supervised Release – A Great Option

When a violent sexual predator is released from incarceration and sent back to the community, the concern has always been what is the potential for reoffending? How dangerous is this person? Because of the nature of the person's crime and the concern for the safety of the public, the pertinent question is what precautions should be taken to protect the citizens, especially if the offender has a record of violence and abuse of children? Of course, that is one of the purposes of the sex offender registries: to make sure known sex offenders are monitored one way or another. But that well intended tool is like a screwdriver with no handle – it doesn't work especially well.

There is a practical option now: supervised release for sex offenders (more in the following pages), with guidelines coming from the Maine Supreme Court that make sense. Recently the high court, for the first time, outlined the factors a judge must consider before imposing supervised release when a sex offender (or other potential reoffender) returns to the community. The court's decision focused on what the sentencing court should consider when determining the length of supervised release. In their opinion decided on August 25, 2011, the high court wrote in the case, State of Maine V. Benjamin S. Cook, the following, *"Like Congress, the Legislature has prescribed statutory considerations applicable to all criminal sentences in Maine, and, like the corresponding federal statute, those considerations include factors apart from direct punishment of the substantive offense. They include*

1. *To prevent crime through the deterrent effect of sentences, the rehabilitation of convicted persons, and the restraint of convicted persons when required in the interest of public safety;*
2. *To encourage restitution in all cases in which the victim can be compensated and other purposes of sentencing can be appropriately served;*
3. *To minimize correctional experiences which serve to promote further criminality;*
4. *To give fair warning of the nature of the sentences that may be imposed on the conviction of a crime; [and] (5 & 6 not relevant)*
5. *To promote the development of correctional programs which elicit the cooperation of convicted persons.*

In addition, a sentencing court is to consider in every felony case the character of the offender and the offender's criminal history …and the protection of the pubic interest.

Given the genesis of Maine's supervised release statute in its federal counterpart and the similarity in purpose between the two, we adopt the federal approach that requires a court, when imposing a term of supervised release and determining its length, to consider statutory sentencing factors appropriate to its primary purpose of supervision and rehabilitation. Guided by those considerations, the court may then impose any conditions of supervised release authorized by (statutory reference) that it deems reasonable and appropriate."(f31)

Therefore, the court's action in issuing these guidelines sets in motion a reliable procedure for all sentencing courts. Cook's guilty pleas and resulting convictions included eleven counts of gross sexual assault (Class A), one count of gross sexual assault (Class A), one count of unlawful sexual contact (Class B), and one count of unlawful sexual contact (Class C). The Superior Court in Knox County imposed an aggregate sentence of twelve years in prison followed by thirty years of supervised release. (f31) Cook appealed the 30 year supervised release requirement and the Supreme Judicial Court ordered that the lower court reconsider that part of the sentence. In February 2012, Superior Court Justice Jeffrey Hjelm reaffirmed the 30 supervised release sentence and elaborated on the reasons for imposing the long sentence. Justice Hjelm said the 30 years of supervision was appropriate and would motivate Cook to follow rules and laws when released from prison.

Supervised release is a vitally important tool for keeping track of sexually violent criminals after they have been released from prison. Lawmakers for several years have been concerned about finding a way to maintain oversight of these dangerous offenders, and as a result the Maine Legislature passed a law in 2000 that allowed judges to impose terms of supervised release on those who are considered to be violent predators.

Benjamin Cook is a good example of why supervised release is so important. In Cook's appeal the court gave a clear explanation of his specific crimes, thus reinforcing the need for continual supervision. The details of his offenses were stated as follows:

> "On February 23, 2010, the State filed a thirty-nine-count information against Cook that included the fourteen counts to which he later entered guilty pleas at a hearing ... .

> The report included the results of interviews conducted with Cook and his two sisters by Knox County Sheriff's Department as a result of a referral made by the Department of Health and Human Services. In summary, Cook's sister described many instances, beginning in 2004 when she was about age five and Cook about seventeen, of hand to genital contact, including occasions when Cook made her masturbate him and he digitally penetrated her vagina; oral sex that he made her perform on him; and genital to genital contact not

involving penetration. The sexual abuse was still ongoing in October 2009.

Cook's other sister reported that he began sexually abusing her when she was age seven and he was about twelve. She described many instances of oral sex that she performed on him and he on her; digital penetration of her vagina; and genital to genital contact involving attempted penetration. The abuse continued until she was age fourteen and he was nineteen. At various times when she resisted him or said she would tell someone what he was doing, he threatened to kill her or rape her in her sleep using a knife. The investigator interviewed Cook twice; he admitted to the conduct described by his sisters." (f31)

Simply releasing people who have committed these types of abuses on children and have threatened death or personal harm to the children cannot be tolerated. Research shows that incarceration will probably not rehabilitate perpetrators with these tendencies and that society deserves greater protection. Placement on the sex offender registry provides some basic information to all interested people, but that system provides limited data about the individual regarding the potential of reoffending.

Supervised release can be imposed for any period of time, including life. It's a relatively newly used concept in Maine, which is why the high court issued the new guidelines for the sentencing courts to follow. It should be noted that there is a distinct difference between probation and supervised release. Probation is meant to be part of the punishment and is included in the sentencing of the offender. Supervised release is designed to monitor and supervise the offender on a continual basis following release from prison because of the recognized potential danger of the perpetrator. The Maine law that authorizes supervised release provides that the court in imposing a sentence of a term of imprisonment cannot include probation in that sentence. Supervised release can only be applied to a non-probation sentence. Therefore, in those cases where supervised release is determined necessary by the court, probation cannot be included as part of the sentence.

It also should be noted that many people confuse probation with parole – two distinctly different applications. Maine no longer uses parole, which is essentially an early release from a predetermined sentence of incarceration. Parole was an incentive used to promote good behavior while in prison, but it proved to be problematic in many ways. Currently, good behavior may be applied in a reduction of a sentence served by as much as a third. Joseph Tellier, the predator who sexually assaulted Michelle Tardif, is a good example of one who was released early because of "good behavior" while incarcerated. To be clear, probation is established as part of the original sentence imposed by the court and has certain restrictions associated with this condition. For example, a prison sentence may be imposed for the possession of online child pornography for six years with all but three years suspended accompanied with a probationary period following incarceration during which time the released offender would be prohibited from having access to a computer. A violation of a probationary requirement can result in being sent back to prison to serve the remainder of the original sentence, which in this example would be the suspended three years.

Step three of the Plan pledges to monitor and support the supervised release option for the sentencing courts including introducing legislation when and where needed. The Maine Supreme Judicial Court issued a well thought out procedure for implementation. Supervised release is another tool for the courts to use when trying to protect society from high-risk offenders who are released into the community. Current probationary procedures are problematic because monitoring offenders is usually categorical; general restrictions and guidelines required of the released offender may be based on the crime committed rather than on other unique factors associated with the individual offenders.

The process is driven by costs. Individualizing each case may be more appropriate, but would be far more costly. Such an explanation is not a justification – just reality.

CHAPTER 7

THE MAINE COMPUTER CRIMES UNIT – THE WAY LIFE SHOULD BE

Step Four – Proper Funding

THE MAINE Computer Crimes Unit plays a vital role in rescuing sexually abused children as was detailed in Chapter Five. The CCU is literally a lifesaver for hundreds of children who are filmed and photographed for pornographic use online. The CCU's record of accomplishments goes right to the core of what citizens and lawmakers alike agree is the most important function of government – rescuing and protecting our children. Legislators and others like to "talk the talk," but too often those in influential positions don't "walk the walk." Interestingly, the lack of focus on the importance of the Computer Crimes Unit is not a reflection of individual governors' concerns or interests, but rather it is a philosophy of the immediate department administrators who over the years have established other priorities within their area of responsibilities, thus treating the CCU as a gnawing responsibility like the live-in mother-in-law or a bothersome tooth that you can't forget about.

Given the importance of the work done by the Computer Crimes Unit, gaining the respect and prestige within the department over the years has been a challenge and a struggle. Hopefully this book will open some eyes to the significant role this unit plays in the daily battle to rescue kids.

The most disturbing and shameful fact, certainly not well known, is that the CCU has gathered valuable forensic evidence from confiscated personal computers containing videos and pictures of severe sexual abuse of children, infants and toddlers. This is critical evidence that would quickly lead to arrests and prosecutions of pedophiles and associated organizations and would take some child predators off the streets and away from their unsuspecting victims. Sadly, this proof of child sexual abuse is sitting in a storage room, waiting for a visit from common sense. Why is this crucial evidence not being processed? Because there are not enough staff at the Computer Crimes Unit to keep up with the important analysis of the computer hard drives that contain the evidence, evidence that is begging for attention.

Maine's Computer Crimes Unit has four forensic examiner positions and has, as of February, 2012, 560 pieces of evidence in their backlog. That means 560 potential/probable sexual predators are still on the streets seeking out new potential victims and/or continuing the current abuse of a child. Why? Because the state government has not provided the necessary basic trained staff to get the available evidence processed to allow prosecution to be initiated. Depending on the size of the various waiting hard drives, it could take anywhere from six months to over a year to clear the backlog -- and that's without taking on any new cases that will continue to add to the backlog. Because of this delay, known predators remain at large for up to a year in most cases in an effort to avoid running up against due process issues. This delay leaves the most dangerous predators at large.

One of the most prominent cases that best illustrates the need to address the forensic backlog is that of Somer Thompson, the little Florida girl whose body was found in a Georgia landfill. Jarred Harrell, who currently awaits trial for the abduction, rape and murder of Thompson, had a computer with a video he had produced allegedly showing Harrell raping his 3-year-old niece. This crucial evidence was sitting on a law enforcement office shelf waiting for a forensic exam two months before he allegedly abducted and murdered the young girl. Harrell was at large as his laptop sat in the forensic backlog closet, thus enabling him to target Somer. Maine needs to make sure this type of needless tragedy is not repeated here in our state – and it is a concern for other states as well.

It is bewildering and frankly unconscionable, that our government leaders would allow evidence of this nature, which is available for processing, to sit untouched twenty feet from an empty desk in the Computer Crimes Unit's headquarters. The general public really has no idea about this deplorable situation, but when the facts become known and people realize that pedophiles and sex offenders are being allowed to continue plotting and engaging in sexual abuses on children simply because someone decided not to hire two extra detectives to analyze the evidence, faces will be red. The embarrassing question that will be asked by both the public and the media will be, "What were you thinking? What were you waiting for all of these years?" Why would the state knowingly let these child sexual abusers continue on unscathed and undeterred, as they plan and implement their next movements either online or by seeking out young victims as their next targets for achieving sexual gratification? It all comes down to a willingness to admit there has been a gross neglect by our government in this area. But there is time to make the changes necessary – and that time is now. This is a human rights issue for children so why aren't we aggressively pursuing the obvious solution? Why?

This proposed plan properly funds the Computer Crimes Unit allowing them to secure and process evidence in a timely manner, thus eliminating the unacceptable backlog that currently exits. This will require State funding within the regular biennial budget for the CCU that will be consistent and dependable as opposed to the current funding procedure of scratching for undependable federal grants just to "get by." Federal grants, because they are so unreliable, sometimes cause harmful disruptions to investigations when valuable trained staff are laid off due to the termination of funding, leaving a void that cannot be filled with the remaining skeletal staff. A detailed explanation of the budget approach is forthcoming.

Step Five - Computer Crimes Unit Upgraded (Not Even Listed Now)

An indicator of the obvious lack of prominence of the Computer Crimes Unit within the Department of Public Safety (DPS) is underscored by its conspicuous absence from the DPS home page website. The homepage lists all 10 Bureaus within the department from Building Codes and Standards to Highway Safety. Even the seven sub-listings in the Bureau of the State Police do not mention the CCU. Polygraph Licensing to Gaming, but no CCU listed anywhere. This lack of presence and recognition speaks volumes about the stature of the Computer Crimes Unit within the Department of Public Safety over the years. Even though it is not displayed prominently, the CCU can be found online by searching under the heading, *Maine Computer Crimes Unit.* The only information available on that site is a less than impressive description of the unit outlined in a three-paragraph narrative that fails to thoroughly present the important role and critical functions of the Unit. It is a critical piece of the Department of Public Safety, yet, it is almost invisible as a department function and is conspicuously absent from the department's organizational structure, an omission that indicates its a priority within the administration. This simply does not make sense and it is time for a change. Appropriate recognition should not be delayed any longer.

The proposed plan changes the Computer Crimes Unit from its current "unlisted" status within the Department of Public Safety. As with all of the significant budget categories within the State Police budget, the CCU should have a visible place in the budget as well (which it doesn't have currently). This change will allow legislators to automatically review the CCU's operations, as they do all other accounts, and will keep this important Unit and its needs in the forefront of those who appropriate funding when creating the state budget every two years. The invisibility of the Computer Crimes Unit over the years has been a significant contributor to its lack of funding by the budget makers.

Lastly, The Most Important Part of the Plan
Step 6 – The Computer Crimes Unit and Associated Laws

The following is a summary of the details of the proposals of Step 6 of the Plan:

1. Make Maine the first state in the union to bring state child exploitation penalties up to a national (federal) standard;
2. Improve Maine's ability to rescue children from ongoing sexual abuse and exploitation by securing desperately needed funds for the Maine Computer Crimes Bureau; and
3. Adjust Maine's criminal code pertaining to child sex abuse by creating more appropriate penalties for predators who sexually abuse children.

Bringing Maine's child exploitation laws up to the national standards requires a careful approach but should definitely be done sooner rather than later. The flourishing black market for video and images of children being raped, tortured, and sexually displayed is one of the greatest human crises facing the United States. According to the National Association to Protect Children (NAPC), testimony before Congress by the U.S. Department of Justice, the FBI, and leading national law enforcement experts, there are hundreds of thousands of individuals in the U.S who are actively engaged in the trafficking of these crime scene recordings. Estimates of the magnitude of this U.S. child exploitation market, including buyers, sellers, and viewers - range from 300,000 to over a million.

"Daddy – Please Stop!"

Contrary to popular misconceptions, the child abuse images trafficked widely on the Internet are not "innocent" or "cute naked children in the bathtub" types of photographs. A large survey (f40) of law enforcement agencies showed the following about the possessors of these videos and images who are arrested by police:

- *83% collect images of children aged 6 -12;*
- 39% collect images of children aged 3 – 5;
- 19% collect images of children aged under 3;
- 80% collect images showing sexual penetration of the child;
- 21% collect images showing children being tortured;
- 1% limit their collections to images of simple nudity;

Renowned Canadian child exploitation expert, Detective Paul Gillespie put it this way: "We regularly seize hundreds of thousands of images of children as young as babies in diapers. There are now 3- and 4 year-olds in 20-minute movies screaming for daddy to stop. This is the norm."(f32)

Different states have different laws and with corresponding penalties pertaining to child sexual exploitation. Thus, a violent sex offender who rapes a child and records the attack on film and places it on the Internet permanently, faces different levels of legal prosecution depending on which state the perpetrator resides. Likewise, a pedophile who "collects" theses videos and probably has engaged in peer to peer sharing could, according to Maine law, easily face as little as probation compared to 5-10 years in a federal court.

Federal penalties exceed state penalties in crimes of child exploitation in almost every instance. This has resulted in a nationwide problem where local and state prosecutors universally and routinely look to federal authorities to prosecute their exploitation cases. In many jurisdictions, the disparity between state and federal sentencing is so great that the local law enforcement agencies have come to see child pornography as a "federal matter." States have large caseloads of local pedophiles caught in possession of child abuse images and local law enforcement agencies often seek assistance from federal prosecutors, hoping to convince them to take their most dangerous cases.(f32)

There should be more consistency among the states, but that will not happen until state legislators decide that these children deserve more protection and make it happen. States should strive to bring their child exploitation sentencing practices up to a single, strong national standard. Despite the popularity of "tough talk" by lawmakers of both political parties, to date, no state has seriously attempted or achieved parity. Maine could be the first and become a national model for the nation.

When this proposal, in the form of legislation, is presented to the Maine Legislature, some lawmakers will say the proposed sentences are too punitive, even though the proposed laws will be the same as existing federal standards. Others will say the increased costs will be too high. But if the same tough talking legislators really believe in a strong pro-child stance and are serious about protecting their human rights, then supporting the adoption of a single set of national standards will be successful in Maine.

Putting this bill together will involve collaboration with several professional organizations. Among them are the National Association to Protect Children (NAPC), the Child Exploitation and Obscenity Section (CEOS) of the U.S. Justice Department, and the National Center for the Prosecution of Child Abuse (a division of the National District Attorney Association). The NAPC shows a comparison of sentencing disparities between Maine laws and federal laws that will give the average person reason to ask the obvious question: why is Maine so lenient when it comes to issuing penalties on sexual offenders? A few examples below illustrate this point.

In Maine the possession of sexually explicit material of children (child pornography) under the age of 12 carries a sentence of 1-5 years. Compare this to the federal sentence for the same crime of 1-10 years. The penalty for solicitation of a child under the age of 12 by computer – trying to make arrangements with a child for sexual purposes – in Maine is 1-5 years compared to the federal penalty of 10 years to life. In Maine sexual exploitation of a minor - producing videos and photographs of sexual abuse of children under the age of 12 – carries a penalty of 1-30 years whereas the federal penalty is 15-30 years. These disparities clearly show why state law enforcement authorities prefer federal prosecution of their more serious sexual abuse cases because of the guarantee of more appropriate sentencing. The perpetrators, on the other hand, always prefer to be prosecuted under state law and the reason is obvious.

The following question needs to be asked. Knowing what is involved in producing videos and pictures of young children who are sexually abused and tortured, do you believe that it is justifiable for a perpetrator to serve just one year in prison, or even two or five, given the crime committed? That could very well happen under existing Maine law. There will be hand wringing and concerns that "it's going to cost too much money" to incarcerate these criminals if sentences are significantly increased. So what does it cost now to watch and worry about these offenders every day they are on the street? What does it cost the child who becomes one of their next victims?

As far as funding is concerned, Maine, along with other states, has a severe lack of resources available to law enforcement for detecting and interdicting child exploitation. Enforcement costs money; there has to be a commitment from the State demonstrating the high priority of protecting children from sexual abuse and rescuing those being sexually assaulted or abused. Therefore, creating a dedicated revenue source for anti-child exploitation task forces and Internet Crimes Against Children (ICAC) task forces is a vital first step. The U.S. Department of Justice's designated Internet Crimes Against Children Task Force (ICAC) in Maine is the Computer Crimes Unit under the Maine State Police.

According to the U.S. Department of Justice, child pornography crimes have *increased 2,500%, becoming the fastest growing crime in America.* Technology today provides law enforcement agencies with the tools to identify and locate sexual predators with pinpoint accuracy. In 2008, data compiled by law enforcement agencies indicated that 2,155 individual computers in Maine had been identified as trafficking in the most hardcore images and movies of infants and toddlers being tortured and raped. (f32)

Enough pounding on the chest and making strong statements about the need to protect kids, especially during election season. Now is the time to finally do something; action needs to be taken to establish the State's commitment to finally address this serious problem.

Want more compelling reasons for the State to provide appropriate funding to fight these worsening attacks on kids? The National Association to Protect Children has stated that based on recent studies of child pornography possessors, the majority are actual hands on offenders, dispelling long held beliefs that offenders who possess and traffic in images are not a threat to children. In September 2011, a bus driver in New Hampshire was arrested for having thousands of images of children being sexually abused. The suspect, John Allen Wright, 45, of Milton, New Hampshire, was arrested on six counts of possession of child pornography and charged with sexually assaulting a disabled 6-year-old boy he was driving to a camp for special-needs children. The assaults are alleged to have taken place in July 2011. There may have been other victims as well. The New Hampshire Internet Crimes Against Children (ICAC) Task Force identified the boy from videos stored in a computer belonging to Wright. This was another important victory for an ICAC. (f33)

In 2010, The U.S. Department of Justices Office of Juvenile Justice and Delinquency Prevention (OJJDP) reported that out of 5,400 arrests of Internet offenders, 2,100 local child victims were identified and rescued.

Now more than ever before child predators are more visible and can be tracked while in the process of searching for young victims. With the appropriate number of trained professional law enforcement officers outfitted with current technological tools, these pedophiles can be traced to their personal residences, often ending a horrendous nightmare for innocent children. In the past these predators had little to fear regarding detection because advanced technology was something in the future. Today, however, the technology is available and now the most significant deterrent for apprehending the offender is proper funding to hire the needed trained professionals. It can no longer be ignored and, in fact, needs to be shouted from the very top of the Maine State Capitol Building while standing on the shoulders of the statue of the draped female figure (as referred to by many), Minerva, Goddess of Wisdom: *The Maine Computer Crimes Unit provides the single greatest prevention against child sexual abuse in Maine's history!*

The best way to approach the funding issue is to create a Computer Crimes Unit funding line in the budget. The funding should come from the State General Fund and should include the same process used to review and evaluate all other "important" agencies and departments. Maine's current General Fund budget for the fiscal years 2012 -13 is *$6.5 billion.* Approximately 80% of this budget funds just two departments, Education and Health and Human Services. The remaining 20% funds all of the other state agencies with the exception of the Department of Transportation that has its own Highway Fund budget.

$6.5 billion ...Billion! If protecting kids and rescuing children that are being sexually abused cannot reach the necessary level of a spending priority, then lawmakers and government officials are not doing what they are preaching. Additional funding can also come from asset forfeitures obtained by the CCU, and a "penalty for offenders" can be assessed as part of each sentencing for sex crimes. Full payment of these fines would be required before the offender would be released from incarceration, thus providing the incentive for the offender to make the appropriate payment. The amount of the penalty would be based on the severity of the crime.

The Six-Point Plan described above is bold and will provide law enforcement agencies, in particular the Computer Crimes Unit, the needed personnel, technology and improved statutes all with the intent of rescuing and protecting young children from sexual abuse. The proposed plan was presented to the Maine Legislature in February 2012, in the form of legislation that is summarized as the follows:

. Creating a new Tier system for the Maine Sex Offender Registry

. Requiring understandable terminology on the sex offender registry

. Reinforces and highlights the supervised release provisions

. Creating a funding line in the General Fund Budget for the CCU.
Bringing Maine's sentencing for sexual offenses against children
   closer to federal sentencing for similar crimes

The vision of this chapter is to identify the broken parts of the sex offender registry and to offer options to restructure the Maine Computer Crimes Unit. These changes will enable maximum efficiency in the CCU's efforts to rescue children from the horrors of sexual assaults and increase the success rate of apprehending pedophiles before other young victims are captured and abused. The CCU must be commended for the unbelievable discipline they have demonstrated during periods of frustration, especially when administrations and lawmakers (except those legislators who have visited the CCU) over the past years seemed not to appreciate the Unit's invaluable work. The hope is that this book unequivocally demonstrates the value of the Computer Crimes Unit and articulates the reasons why proper funding and administrative support are essential if rescuing children is, in fact, government's top priority. Informing the public and influential leaders about the critical work done by the CCU is definitely a top priority of this chapter. The goal is quite simple: rescue as many of the sexually tortured and abused children as possible and remove those who prey on children for sexual gratification from the streets ….for a long time.

Maine has an opportunity to be a national leader in saving children's lives and capturing evil predators who steal the souls and hearts of the innocent and vulnerable. Maine can and should lead the way. What a great time to follow our State's motto "Dirigo" and set a new direction for ourselves and for our children.

CHAPTER 8

AN INTERVIEW WITH A
CONVICTED CHILD PORN ADDICT

How and Why He Got Into Online Child Pornography

GIVE DAVID a machete and point him towards a large pile of snow and he would, in what seemed almost like magic, transform the indistinguishable heap of frozen slush into an impressive and award winning snow sculpture. The end results of his creativity were exact replicas of popular cartoon characters like Charlie Brown, Goofy, Mickey and Minnie. Add the appropriately placed food coloring that highlighted their well-known features and presto – the snow characters came to life with perfection.

David's fraternity at Gorham State College was the beneficiary of his unusual talent and his Kappa Delta Phi brothers proudly accepted the campus snow sculpture competition crown nearly every year that he was wielding the knife and attacking the wintery pile. David was not a "Big Man On Campus" or BMOC. Even his popularity in the fraternity and accompanying annual winter notoriety did not thrust him into the social scene as one might expect. He was quiet, followed all the rules and was usually the designated driver at the fraternity drinking parties. He was more reserved, "kind of a watcher," as he now defines himself 40 years later. That trait stayed with him as he progressed through life achieving success and prominence: he was "kind of a watcher."

David grew up on a small farm in Windham, Maine, and came from a family of service men, including his great, great uncle, David Chapman, who was a Civil War veteran and for whom David was named. The family history of military service probably influenced his decision to enlist in the U.S. Navy after completing college. At that time the Vietnam War was winding down; however, every young man was facing the military draft, and by enlisting in the Navy he avoided having to wait to be drafted. Expecting to serve the minimum three years and then be discharged, David decided to reenlist and enter officer Candidate School and was commissioned as an ensign in the U.S. Navy Reserves. After a 23-year career, David retired with a rank of Commander in the U.S. Navy.

Retiring from the Navy at such a relatively young age offered opportunities for a second career, and he decided to follow his college training and became a teacher. David's interest was in the field of science so becoming a high school science teacher suited him very well. His teaching career lasted for 12 years and during that time David was elevated to the position of Head Teacher and was assigned to teach honors and advanced placement classes. Once again he had achieved success earning the respect of his collegues and the confidence of his supervisors.

Throughout the years another interest had captivated his imagination - photographing nude women. David was involved in nude photography while in the Navy as he traveled and visited various countries around the world. His travels took him to places where opportunities to expand his special photography interests were abundant. In some ways things had not changed since his youth – he still liked to watch from somewhat of a distance.

When computers became part of the American life style, David easily transitioned his traditional voyeurism into the endless world of online pornography websites, thus becoming an avid watcher. His attraction to pornography evolved into more than just the usual male interest in female nudity and the usual adult pornography. David not only viewed these sites, but he actually downloaded the various pictures and videos onto disks to save for later viewing. He became a "collector" and organized the images into categories of women such as redheads, blondes, brunettes, and created certain specialties among his collection such as highlighting certain physical features of women like a collage of women's breasts. David had carefully designed a user-friendly library of pornography from which he could conveniently make selections choosing from a wide variety of images based on his sexual desires at any given moment. "That went on for several years from 1996 to 2002," David said. He said his wife and daughter were aware that he was visiting the sites and "didn't consider it a necessarily unhealthy situation. I had a pretty large collection – 8000 to 10,000 images," David recalls. "Kind of a watcher," as he defined himself, could be an understatement.

He Crossed the Line

After several years of visiting thousands of porn sites the excitement lessened and admittedly that activity became boring. "There came a point when much of what I was doing was mundane," David said. He started searching for different and more interesting and stimulating sites. David discovered the photographic work of David Hamilton, a controversial photographer who is known for using children in sexually suggestive poses as the subjects of some of his work. Hamilton's work probably influenced David's private fascinations. David became attracted to viewing photos and videos online of nude and nearly nude younger children. He remembers receiving an email inviting him to a site that showed images of pubescent girls who were skimpily clothed and sexually suggestive. The site had a disclaimer stating that the images were legal; however, David said that was the "hook" because embedded in that web page were offerings to go to other sites. "I guess I thought about it (going to those illegal sites) for a quite a while. I was kind of bored with what I had been doing. I crossed the line, I admit it. I knew it was wrong and I did it anyway," David recalled.

As has been documented in earlier chapters, participating in online visits leaves a trail revealing a user's interests and habits. In the case of child pornography invitations to introductory "legal" sites are individualized based on one's previous online visitation history that is easily available to special interest groups. Once at the site other more intriguing invitations are made available to the visitor. It's true that the child porn industry uses slick and well tested methods to attract potential paying clients and the best way for them to make that connection is to start with a legal, but suggestive site, and then offer more explicit images. All they need is a credit card number.

The child porn sites that David said he visited showed children of a range of ages from very young - that David says were not of interest to him, to pubescent age children that *were* the focus of his interest. Entry into these illegal sites requires payment and the easiest method of paying is to use a credit card. He had to make the payment through a neutral organization, another precautionary measure employed by the child porn industry designed to protect their identity. Unfortunately, for those who use their credit cards to subscribe to these sites, the trail is relatively easy to follow back to the owner of the card. These neutral collection organizations guarantee to protect the purchaser's identity and that all personal data, including credit card information is secured. Anonymity is guaranteed! Want to buy a bridge?

"I got into one site – advertised as a Russian site - that was certainly darker than the others and even though the models were of the same age, they were dirty, abused, and bruised – [they had] the vacant stares. I basically said to myself, "What the hell are you doing here?" By buying into this site you're paying for this abuse," David recalled in a depressed and embarrassed manner. He had crossed the line and had willingly lowered himself into the dark world of helpless and frightened children who were sexually assaulted for the sole purpose of pleasing and gratifying the paying customers. David was there! He was watching. He was a paying customer.

David said that viewing the Russian site and seeing the abused children who were serving as the "models" is when the realization hit him that he had become a contributor to the abuse. One could reasonably wonder why it took so long to realize the obvious. Regardless, he said that he shut down all of the child porn sites and got rid of the adult porn sites too. "I still had my collection (downloaded porn images of adults and children) and was reticent to get rid of that," he said. After deleting all of his pornography sites from his computer David still knew that he had done something wrong and that gnawing fear stayed with him as he went on with his life, living what he would later learn in his sex offender treatment class was called "pretend normal."

In the spring of 2002 David had his computer "wiped clean" at a local computer repair shop and felt more relieved that any evidence of his illegal activities would be gone forever. "I breathed a little bit more normal," he remembered knowing that his illegal computer trail was covered. As we have learned, "wiped clean" is an assumption that should not be made – especially if prosecution is a possibility waiting in the wings.

And Then It Happened

In June 2003 while driving into his driveway on the way home from school a large black Chevy Suburban with federal license plates pulled in behind him and two guys got out. They asked his name and if he knew anything about a particular online pornography site and David said that he did not recognize the site name. After a few more questions the two men, both federal agents, told David why they were there. The men presented a large three-ring binder containing David's complete history, financial and otherwise, that included his credit card records. The credit card payments to several illegal child porn sites, including the Russian site, were listed. The United States had been working with foreign governments, including Russia, trying to locate and arrest those who were participating in the site. Russian child porn sites tend to be especially vulgar and dangerous in terms of hardcore abuse to children. Remember the "snuff" child pornography videos referenced in an earlier chapter were made in Russia.

The federal agents asked if they could look at David's computer and he agreed and let them into the house. Even if he had refused their request it is standard operating procedure for investigating officers in these situations to secure a search warrant prior to arrival at the residence. The warrant allows the agents to not only enter the house, but search for other evidence including downloaded images and materials containing child pornography such as disks and CD's. David's collection that he was so *reticent* to dispose of would become the prime evidence used against him during the prosecution. Once in the house they did not just look at his computer, they seized it in accordance with standard procedure in suspected computer crimes cases. The investigators asked David if he had other child pornography material so he showed them his "collection" of approximately 200 floppy disks and CD's containing the 8,000 to 10,000 images. David knew full well that some of those disks contained illegal child porn images. One might wonder if you take the time to remove from the computer all of the evidence of illegal child porn visits and doing so provides such a sense of relief as David described, then why keep other conclusive and damning evidence like CD's and disks where it can be easily confiscated?

"At that point I was thinking, what did I get myself into?" David recalls. Realizing that the federal agents would discover the many illegal child porn images within his collection, a sick feeling of a very scary future swirled around him then slammed into this gut. David knew that he had to tell his wife and children about what he had done and that federal prosecution was a possibility. As scared and embarrassed as David was for himself and his family, knowing that he contributed to the sexual assault of children around the world was of equal distress and shame. Those who support the online child porn industry by subscribing to the various websites are key financial contributors to the industry. It is they who provide the incentive for the production of online videos and photographs of the rape and torture. Some perpetrators realize the consequences of their involvement and others never really think about it. David was one of those who knew the consequences to the children and -- to himself.

From June 2003, when the federal agents first came to David's house and confiscated his computer, disks, and CD's, until his appearance before a federal judge in January 2008 on the charge of possessing child pornography, nothing much had happened – everything was in limbo. It was during that time that David went back to teaching high school science and living somewhat of a normal life, except he always carried with him the realization that the next phone call, the next knock on the door, the next vehicle pulling into the door yard could be the beginning of the nightmare he had tucked away in his mind for more than four years.

At his January hearing, David said the judge ordered more psychological examinations for him, thus extending his court hearing until August 2008. At that August hearing he pled guilty to one count of possessing child pornography. "I threw myself on the mercy of the court," David said. The evidence against him was solid and David had already admitted to himself and his family that he had "done wrong." He said that agreeing to one count in this case meant admitting to the possession of 10-150 images of illegal child pornography. The judge sentenced him to one year and a day in federal prison. According to David, this particular sentence, since it was literally more than one year, allowed him to take advantage of the good behavior provision in the federal correctional system and, therefore he could be eligible for release in approximately seven months of the original sentence, if all went well.

"You Don't Want to Go There!"

David was sentenced to serve his time at the Metropolitan Correctional Center, a Federal Bureau of Prisons remand center located in New York City adjacent to Foley Square on Park Row in lower Manhattan. This is an administrative facility designed to house federal prisoners who are either pre-trial or on holdover status. The Metropolitan Correction Center is noted for housing dangerous and infamous criminals such as John Gotti, former boss of the Gambino crime family, Jackie D'Amico, another boss of the Gambino crime family, Faisal Shahzard, of the accused Times Square attempted car bomber, Victor Bout, international arms trafficker, and Abduwali Abdukhadair Muse, one of the notorious Somali pirates. Other less dangerous yet very notable inmates like Bernard Madoff were housed at this federal prison. (f34) David's lawyer, who had seen this facility, was especially concerned and told David, "You don't want to go there!"

David hired a consulting agency that specialized in crafting formal requests to the court in support of placing convicted criminals in specific prisons. In this case the request for David to be assigned to an alternate prison was based on the need for a facility with a sex offender treatment program and one that was closer to his family. There are federal prisons in Massachusetts that had the sex treatment programs and certainly were closer to Maine. However, the request was denied by the court and David had to report to the MCC as originally ordered. "So I basically got on a Boston train, rode to prison and turned myself in. It was a tough thing to do. Literally I had to go to the back door of this big (prison), push the button and say here I am," David recalled. He was 62 years old.

Once inside everyone is treated the same, whether you're a crime boss, a terrorist or someone from Maine convicted of possessing child pornography. It makes no difference. The first two weeks David spent in solitary confinement as required of all new inmates. Then he was placed on the second floor where all of the "grunt work" inmates are housed. All are assigned to perform the basic needs of the facility like working in the kitchen, laundry, cleaning, and whatever else was required. David, because of his formal education, worked in the library and instructed education classes, including GED courses, (General Equivalency Diploma). According to David, the general pay was 5 cents per hour.

David said he was never abused or assaulted, but there were occasional rebuffs when others learned of his crime. "There were various groups, ethnic and otherwise, that hung out together on the floor. There were the Hispanics, blacks, mafia, and others. I was grouped with the misfits that nobody cared about or wanted," David said. On occasion he would get comments from other inmates when they learned of his offense, especially from the Hispanic group because, according to David, "Their tolerance would be zero for (child related sex offenders). Even though they might be murderers, bank robbers or anything else, I was lower than they were."

It was difficult for his wife to visit the prison since it required an overnight trip and driving into the city was not a viable option for her. She would travel to Albany to her son's house and then take the train into the city the next day. Both agreed that David could basically do his time, six to seven months, and she would not attempt to make the difficult regular visits. David's goal was try to maintain his sanity and complete his sentence knowing that the next step in the process was placement in a "half-way house" in Portland, Maine.

One morning in July, after a little more than six months in a federal prison, David was given a bus ticket and told to go to a halfway house on Sherman Street in Portland, Maine. In general, halfway houses do not have stellar reputations according to some who have been assigned to complete their sentences at these locations. David said he was told on several occasions by inmates, "I'd rather spend my time here than in a halfway house."

By the time David was released, his hair was long and his grey, bushy beard had grown down to the middle of his chest giving him an almost mid-Eastern appearance as he described it. When he arrived at the halfway house, a complete body search was conducted along with a thorough examination of his belongings. During that search they discovered among his personal materials some Islamic passages David had jotted down pertaining to previous religious discussions with Islamic inmates at MCC – purely academic from his point of view. However, given his appearance and the Islamic quotes, David said he became immediately suspect as a possible terrorist and was asked by the supervisor at the halfway house, "Am I going to have trouble with you?"

He was assigned to a room in the attic that had a small bed with a vinyl-covered sack that served as a mattress. David said that the first and most important concern of those operating the halfway house was to generate enough income to pay the monthly rent. The building was contracted with the federal government and David said money earned by the inmates employed in area jobs during their time at the house provided the necessary income to pay the rent. If rent is not paid, then the inmate is returned to prison. After they discovered that David was on a pension with a reliable income, the concern about paying his monthly rent dissipated and the importance of his finding a paying job was of little concern to the managers of the house. David found a couple organizations that accepted his voluntary services, such as the Red Cross and the Maine Historical Society, which provided a daily routine for him and helped the time go by.

Following David's required three-month assignment at the half-way house, he was finally released from incarceration to go back home to begin his probationary period. While on probation, he was not allowed to consume alcohol, view pornography in any form or be around children under the age of 18. David says he has not seen his young nieces and nephews for years. He did resume his involvement in various local organizations in Windham, including the local veterans and historical groups.

One of the requirements of his probation was to enroll in "The Counseling & Psychotherapy Center, Inc. (CPC) program for sex offenders. David had to sign a contract with the CPC pledging his agreement to abide by the strict mandates and to fulfill all of the responsibilities required as a participant in the program. The Treatment Contract read as follows:

> *It is the goal to help you learn ways to run your life more successfully and to have no more victims. We will provide firm boundaries for your treatment and help you develop self-discipline to help you control your behaviors. We strongly believe that taking steps to preserve community safety will always be in your best interest. We are invested in your success and believe this program can greatly improve your chances for living without a new offense. The choices will always be yours but we will be there to assist you.*

The introductory paragraph explains the purpose of the CPC counseling program. The contract goes on to explain the obligations of the participants including specific restrictions associated with all forms of pornography. Each participant must agree to the following statement: *I accept that while I am in sex offender treatment I will not view or have pornography in my possession.* A couple examples of the long list of restrictions are the following:

- *I agree not to keep any pictures of naked children or children in their underwear.*
- *I agree not to possess any pictures of children I do not know or any pictures of children that could be seen as erotic.*

Each participant must agree to take at least two physically related tests if asked: the polygraph test to confirm a level of honesty necessary for successful treatment of sex offenders, and the penile plethysmograph or phallometry test used to assess sexual patterns of sex offenders. The penile plethysmograph (pluh-THIZ-muh-graph) is a machine used for measuring changes in the circumference of the penis. A stretchable band containing mercury is fitted around the subject's penis. The band is connected to a machine with a video screen and data recorder. Any changes in the penis size, even those not felt by the subject, are recorded while the subject views sexually suggestive or pornographic pictures, slides, or movies, or listens to audio tapes with descriptions of such things as children being molested.

Computer software is used to develop graphs showing "the degree of arousal to each stimulus." The machine was developed in Czechoslovakia to prevent draft dodgers from claiming they were gay just to avoid military duty. (f35)

The reliability of the penile plethysmograph test has been challenged by opponents of the process who believe that the test is flawed and the results should not be used to assess the sexual interests of the subjects. There are also concerns about the appropriateness of requiring people to submit to these tests from a civil liberties point of view. Regardless of the controversy, the test is used to provide insight about the sexual preferences of sex offenders and to measure the subject's sexual interests in specific populations such as children.

David felt the CPC program was essentially inefficient and much time was wasted, thus missing opportunities to provide meaningful help to the individuals in the class. However, criticizing the instructor's approach and the effectiveness of the curriculum was not advised since failure to complete the course requirements, as determined by the instructor, meant a violation of probation and back to prison.

Watching and Touching – Hand in Hand

This chapter provides a real example of someone who had an obsession with pornography as noted by his long hours of viewing thousands of porn sites on his computer. The fact that David developed a virtual porn library by creating a collection of 8,000–10,000 images downloaded onto disks and CDs further illustrated his obsession with pornography. Many people choose to view legal adult pornography online and some people are routine visitors to these sites. The difference between those who view adult porn and those who are attracted to images of children who are sexually assaulted or just nude is significant. Like an alcoholic in a bar, a person with tendencies to view child porn should not be surfing the Internet viewing pornography – even adult porn. David is an example of someone who admitted to having interests in viewing nude or partially nude pubescent age children. His sexual attraction to this age group provided the perfect scenario, after years of viewing and collecting images from adult porn sites, to slip into the devastating world of child porn.

The term "kiddie porn" is not used in this book because of the less than destructive connotation it presents. It is inappropriate to minimize recorded violent sexual assaults on children by using a soft descriptive word like "kiddie." The word "kiddie" is antithetical to the dreadfulness associated with child pornography.

David was adamant that he was never involved with any type of "hands-on" sexual abuse of children. As was documented earlier in this chapter, he admitted that by subscribing to the child porn sites, he was supporting the sexual abuse of children. Many people, including some sex offenders who have discussed their personal cases, feel that merely viewing child porn is innocuous and is not harmful. Some advocate that making such an activity illegal is a misuse of justice, and laws pertaining to possession of child pornography should to be changed. Such a belief is difficult to comprehend and is an indication that more education and awareness of the child porn industry are necessary.

Acknowledging the serious ramifications of viewing and subscribing to child porn Internet sites is extremely important both by those who possess these images and by society. The child pornography industry is fueled by money from those who like to watch – those who will pay to watch. There are studies that show a high percentage of those who view child porn eventually sexually assault victims. There are child porn subscribers who never sexually assault children, but some studies show that many watchers become, or are already, hands-on abusers. The line between the two types of sexual abuse is thin and blurs easily. Once a person is in the quagmire of child pornography, sinking to further depths is licentiously intoxicating and swift beyond immediate recognition.

Husband and Wife Team - Convicted Sex Offenders Together They Sexually Assaulted A 9 Year- Old Girl

Many sex offenders are not focused on the Internet child pornography world, preferring instead to participate in hands-on sexual assaults of children. The most common category of child sex offenders is adult male although females are sexual offenders as well. The less common category of sexual offenders is a husband and wife or man and woman who jointly sexually assault a victim together as a couple. Remember Stephen and Tina Bickart from Sanford, Maine and their violent sexual assault of the 2-year-old baby.

Christopher and his wife were convicted of gross sexual assault of a 9-year-old girl who happened to be a relative and as a result, she was very trusting of the couple. During an interview in October 2011, Christopher said he and his wife confined their assault to performing oral sex on the girl, and it occurred five to seven times during the period of 1998 and 1999. On some occasions he would assault the girl by himself and other times the crime was committed by both of them. Christopher said the girl's response was passive during the assaults and that violence or threats were not used.

Sex offenders may have a preference as to gender and age levels. Technically speaking, those who are sexually attracted to prepubescent children are referred to as pedophiles. Those who prefer pubescent children, between the ages of 11–14, are defined as hebephiles. Generally sex offenders do not restrict their assaults to just their favorite age group since availability can be an overriding factor. "While I was attracted to girls of the teenage years, the closest thing I had available was my younger victim," said Christopher. Availability can easily trump preference.

Christopher explained that the term "grooming," as he learned in his sex offender treatment program, is defined as "the actions taken leading up to a sexual assault." Getting the victim in a cooperative state of mind allows the predator to act out the assault with greater ease. As mentioned, in Christopher's case the young victim was a relative, and because a level of trust had been established between the girl and the couple, initiating the assaults was relatively easy. Still, grooming takes time even with previously established relationships. Trust, confidence, reliability, and caring are the tools of the predator as he or she works to create the right moment to initiate the actual sexual assault.

Christopher admits, "The older she got and the more she began to develop I think I was preparing for long term grooming. In my mind I loved her and it would be okay - I'm not hurting her. I knew it was wrong, but it will be okay because of love and passion and caring. Yes, I will be fulfilling a deviant need of mine, but it will be done in a respectful way." Such is a real example of the rationale of a sex offender's inner mind that is ratcheted up to justify the planned and carefully strategized sexual assault of an unsuspecting victim. Through Christopher's involvement in the post incarceration mandatory sex treatment program, he is able to verbalize his thoughts and rationalizations leading up to the time of the assaults. His willingness to openly discuss his deviant behavior provides an opportunity for you, the reader, to get a glimpse, albeit brief, into the mind of a sexual predator. Incorporating the emotions of love, caring and passion while sexually assaulting a child is a convenient manipulation that allows the sex offenders to complete the sexual gratification. Not only do the predators groom their victims, they must groom themselves in preparation for committing the act.

Grooming the parents is equally important in the overall plan, and they can be easy targets for the experienced and calculating sexual predator. As we have established in previous chapters, it's not the stranger lurking in the dark shadows that should be the predominant concern of parents. Such a naïve belief is misleading and dangerously disarming. More likely, the predator is well known by the victim and the victim's family. Over 90% of sexual assaults on children are committed either by a family member, a family friend or a family acquaintance. The grooming of parents allows the child to be literally handed over to the pedophile to do with as he pleases. Parents and adults who supervise children need to be aware of the sophistication and tactics used by today's sexual predators. Times have changed with new technology and the billion-dollar online child porn industry driving the need for a continual supply of children for filming and for photographing, and for sale.

Christopher and his wife both pled guilty in 2003 to sexually assaulting the young girl and were sentenced to 7 years in prison with all but 2 years suspended. They both served 20 months in prison getting early release due to the standard "good time" that is part of most Corrections systems. Their probations will be completed in December 2012, at which time Christopher will have completed his sex treatment program. His wife's sex treatment requirements have been completed.

Christopher currently works as a part-time flagger and makes less than $8,000 a year and his wife has a small crafts business that he says does not provide a suitable income. As a sex offender convicted of gross sexual assault, Christopher is required to be a lifetime registrant on the sex offender registry. When interviewing for various jobs, he says that once the prospective employer knows that Christopher is a sex offender (required), the interview essentially ends. No one wants to hire someone with a record as a felon and a sex offender. At the age of 48 his future career possibilities look grim although his attitude seems positive given the circumstances.

The couple's victim, according to Christopher, experienced emotional problems throughout her school years; however, he is unaware of her emotional status today. Obviously, the concern for the victim must be the highest priority and hopefully she is able to deal with her tragic experience.

Christopher and his wife must spend the remainder of their lives known as the worst of all felons – sex offenders -- never to be trusted. Christopher explained the reality of what they (he and his wife) can expect for the rest of their lives, "The world is not going to trust me until two days after I die, at which point they'll say, You know what? He actually did live (the remainder) his life as a good person and didn't reoffend. I guess we can cut him a break."

Their victim was an innocent target who was sexually groomed and suffered the consequences of sexual abuse. She deserves the same opportunity to explain her ordeals and tribulations. (However, out of respect for her anonymity, she was not identified or named in this book.) An insightful observation of how a sex offender thinks and acts can be beneficial and should be shared with the public. But the young victims of these assaults need and deserve confidentiality as their recovery progresses.

CHAPTER 9

SEXUAL FETISHES
WHEN THEY GO FROM INNOCENT TO EVIL

PUTTING A computer in the hands of a child porn addict is like bringing an alcoholic to a local bar during happy hour. The temptation to cross the line and indulge in old destructive habits and urges may be uncontrollable. The same applies to certain sexual fetishes that, if controlled and performed in private without inflicting harm, can be acceptable if the respect and rights of others are maintained. However, sexual fetishes can become obsessive, risky and treacherous to both the fetishists and others who may be part of the fantasy. The prevalent concern is that some fetishists may transition their sexual desires and attention to children, and that issue will be examined later in this chapter. Becoming familiar with the various sexual fetishes is educational, interesting, and shocking, in some instances. Part of the process of educating the public about potential dangers to children is to increase awareness of the nontraditional objects or situations that inspire sexual arousal.

For purposes of complete disclosure I want to state that I am not a psychologist, psychiatrist, sex therapist or sex expert of any kind. I have done considerable research on fetishism to make the connection between fetishistic behavior and the need to constantly be aware of the potential danger to children from many directions, fetishism included.

The term *sexual fetish* can be defined in a variety of ways and has different meanings, even to the professionals who have researched the subject extensively. However, the following definition is a combination of several opinions and best serves the purpose of this chapter. Sexual fetish:

"The sexual arousal a person receives from a physical object or from a specific situation. The object or situation of interest is referred to as a fetish." Today a reference to someone having a fetish, such as a foot fetish, may mean only that feet are a sexual turn on. A fetish is considered a disorder when sexual gratification or the ability to perform a sexual act can only be achieved by incorporating the fetish. If a male can only achieve an erection and have an orgasm while engaging in *odaxelagnia,* being bitten by or biting his sexual partner, then he could have a problem. The severity of the condition can be directly related to the particular fetish involved. *Somnophillia*, the desire to watch the sex partner sleep, referred to as "sleeping beauty," could present a serious obstacle to sexual performance especially if the person wants his or her partner to be an active participant in the sex act.

People who have the sexual fetish known as *omolagnia*, "to be sexually aroused by nudity," might be considered to be quite normal, as opposed to someone with a bizarre and hideous fetish known as *anthropophagolagnia*, "the need to rape victims and then eat them," e.g. Jeffrey Dahmer and Ottis Toole. Fetishes that are not harmful to others, including sex partners, may be seen as odd by most people, but generally accepted with a "to each his own" type of attitude in our culture. The more bizarre the sexual fetish, the less they are understood by society. Eyebrows are raised viewing those with the weird fetishes as …well, weird. It is important to remember that if normal sexual performance and gratification cannot be achieved without the use of the fetish, then it's probably a disorder that may need professional attention.

Agalmatophillia is the fetish of those who "enjoy having sex or being involved sexually with mannequins, dolls, or statues." Although not the normal sex partner, this fetish really isn't harmful to others as long as the "never say no" love object is not misused – say, placed in the vehicle passenger seat when taking advantage of the multi-passenger, high speed lane. Considerably more abnormal is the fetish known as *paraphillic,* "men wearing diapers and pretending to be an infant during sexual activity with a partner." Assuming the role of an infant and submitting to domination by the sex partner supposedly releases all responsibilities. Both of these fetishes are certainly seen as peculiar as are the following fetishes: *urophillia*, "sexual arousal by peeing on the sex partner or being peed on and peeing in public;" *eproctophillia,* "sexual arousal from the act of farting;" *emetophillia,* "vomiting on the sex partner or being vomited on during sex;" *acrotomophilia,* "the sexual attraction to people with missing limbs;" *salirophillia,* "getting literally dirty, (mud, grass stains) during sex and putting dirt on the sex partner;" and *ursusagallmatophillia,* "dressing up like animals, sometimes referred to as "furries" and "plushies" while involved in sexual activities."

Beyond the weird category are those fetishes that are on the edge and can easily become harmful and potentially fatal: *Hematolagnia,* involving the "use of blood during sex including drinking and in some cases collecting blood;" *necrophillia,* "being sexually attracted to corpses and/or having intercourse with corpses;" and *hybristophillia,* "the attraction, usually by a female, to convicted criminals serving time for horrific crimes, sometimes the more heinous the crime the greater the attraction." We often read about the most dangerous criminals such as Charles Manson and several others who are incarcerated receiving written marriage proposals from women. Convicted felons who are serving life sentences for torturing, sexually assaulting, and murdering women are examples of people this type of fetishist (usually females) would be attracted to.

When Body Parts are Covered

Sexual fetishes can transition from motivational to pathological depending on the psychological condition of the fetishists. The perceived innocence of *partialism,* the sexual attraction to specific parts of the body such as feet, toes, hair (particularly red hair), legs, ears, breasts, and buttocks can be of concern if combined with other disorders. For example, fetishists who have voyeuristic tendencies and are attracted to looking up skirts and dresses to see panties or buttocks of unsuspecting females are of concern. The standard operating procedure of the "upskirt" fetishist is to carry a concealed video or photographic camera to public locations such as malls or other gathering places of younger females. The "photographer" has a carrying bag that can be lowered below the victim's skirt and tilted upward to get pics and vids of the unknowing female's buttocks and panties. The victim may be walking, standing, especially walking up stairs or standing on escalators, or bent over looking at items on shelves. The fetishists are very creative in positioning the camera at the right time and place. Women and girls who may be sitting in various positions at parades, athletic events, on park benches or getting in and out of vehicles are fertile grounds for the upskirt hunter.

Like many of the more common fetishes, partialism can be considered normal when exercised in a legal and responsible manner: however, when the intention is to view those body parts that are considered private, then such behavior is definitely inappropriate and unacceptable. It should be noted that upskirting, by its very nature, is illegal regardless of the fetish involved.

The same upskirting technique mentioned above is used on children, only the preferred locations for seeking out victims are different. The prime locations for upskirting children are playgrounds where there are an abundance of swings, slides and jungle gyms that provide the ideal opportunity to film the preferred targets. Children are less conscious of their clothing especially when playing on the equipment, resulting in skirts and dresses not just lifted temporarily, but falling over their heads as they hang by their legs on the gym, pump to the sky on the swing and float down the slide. There are those carefully looking for these carefree moments in hopes of taking close-up photos or videos of exposed panties, bottoms, and crotches. Attending adults need to be educated and aware of these types of fetishes and the corresponding vulnerability of children at all times. Children need to be taught to wear proper playground clothing for safety and privacy. The perceived innocence of playing is enjoyable to watch for most people, but to others it is an opportunity to act out a perversion involving innocent children. School playgrounds are no exception and need constant observation when kids are around; however, abundant supervision and limited public access at these play areas reduce the opportunities for the upskirt predator. Schools provide the ideal environment to teach children and adults about appropriate playground attire and awareness.

Upskirting children is another example of intolerable fetishistic behavior that is antithetical to the more common fetishes preferred by adults who carry them out in private and always respect the rights of others. Some of the most popular upskirting targets involving youth are cheerleaders of all ages, especially middle and high school age groups. (Now there are organized cheering for very young children and the interested pedophiles are fully aware of the increasing number of new targets.) There are other situations where innocent and popular activities involving young people can be transformed into sexually suggestive images by a fetishist with a camera and later viewed online by paying child porn enthusiasts. The pictures of girls doing acrobatic jumps, backflips, and cartwheels, feature close-up shots of crotches, always aiming for a slight "clothing malfunction." These photos and videos can be sold to child porn sites where upskirting subscriptions bring in substantial amounts of money to the porn industry. Viewers who have sexual fetishes of voyeurism combined with *partialism* (when acted out illegally) make upskirting one of the most popular Internet sites on the web – and one of the most alarming when innocent children are the unknowing "stars."

The purpose of this chapter is to educate and increase awareness about sexual fetishes and to illustrate how preferences to certain sexual tendencies can be private and consensual. However, it is important for adults to understand that children can become the sexual fetish, thus exposing them to manipulation by evil-minded fetishists whose sole purpose is either self-sexual gratification or money - or both.

There is an increasing potential for children to be sexually abused and misused by omnipresent pedophiles whose creativity and determination for sexual gratification at the expense of innocent children never ends. Fetishism is not a predictor of pedophilic behavior nor does it necessarily present a threat to society although there is that possibility with some fetishists. Parents and adults who supervise children need to be aware of fetishistic behaviors and use that knowledge to protect children from potential victimization. There is a meaningful balance between constant paranoia and naïve security - commonsense and attentiveness are the best approaches as we keep cautious watch over our children.

CHAPTER 10

WHAT IT'S ALL ABOUT
WHERE DO WE GO FROM HERE

THE FUNDAMENTAL basis of the previous nine chapters have the potential to set a new course in establishing enlightened and improved standards for laws to protect our children from sexual assault and to design a system to efficiently manage sex offenders. Learning about victims who as children were subjected to repeated sexual molestation and life threatening sexual assault has helped form a better appreciation for the need for more effective laws. Having a better understanding of the potential of unintended consequences when writing and passing legislation is a lesson we can take from the pages of this book.

We know that too often lawmakers overreact to situations involving sex crimes against children as they clumsily stumble to the front of the demanding masses wanting to demonstrate the leadership expected of elected officials. Albeit well intended, the danger of passing new laws in response to public anger and frustration frequently results in legislation that is void of sound research and tested consequences. We have learned that even commonsense is sometimes a faulty measuring device and that emotion-based legislation is problematic. The current approach appears to fix a void in the law today that leaves a mess in the law tomorrow. Whenever a single circumstance is driving the efforts for a new law or a change in existing law, that should be a red flag to both lawmakers and the public.

Michelle Tardif exposed a serious problem with the sex offender registry and successfully outlined the changes that needed to be made so that people like Joseph Tellier would be placed on the sex offender registry. Remember that it was discovered, after the changes were made, that the new law brought with it a series of damaging impacts that lingered well into the future. Research for this book has revealed that it is a formula for disaster when well-intended legislators feel compelled to work quickly to protect society from dangerous sex offenders. Michelle was right about her concerns and we were wrong in how we addressed them. Her story was captivating and we could not wait to fix the problem that she revealed with the passion of a determined mother. The Criminal Justice and Public Safety Committee could not wait to show its compassion and eagerness to correct a glaring hole in the law - but we should have. We needed the wisdom and strength to slow the process down, be more deliberate and carefully weigh the consequences of our actions.

The committee's decisions turned the lives of undeserving citizens upside down by unnecessarily putting them on the sex offender registry, for their neighbors and the world to see and judge. Some of these people were not the "bad guys" we wanted to get – they were not the Joseph Telliers of the world. The new registrants were living and breathing examples of "unintended consequences" who were required to be placed on the registry as a result of plea agreements made as many as twenty years before. It was a lesson learned and hopefully this book provides guidance to future legislatures and caring lawmakers – like we were.

The road map for important changes to the sex offender registry is now evident as a result of the research compiled for this book. It is obvious that potentially dangerous sex offenders need to be placed in proper view of law enforcement agencies and the concerned public. There is no doubt that most of the 4000 plus sex offender registrants in Maine have been convicted of serious sex offenses and require monitoring in varying degrees. However, it is now apparent that the public needs to know the degree of concern each registrant deserves. Instituting a tier system, as outlined in this book, within the sex offender registry is imperative in an effort to provide an effective guide for the user. Distinguishing between the various levels of sex offenders on the registry allows for a more accurate understanding of the crimes committed by each registrant. We now have a game plan to improve the sex offender registry that should be implemented by the Legislature as soon as possible.

The William Elliott and Joseph Gray Easter murders in 2006 underscored the necessity of instituting lay terminology as part of the descriptions of offenses displayed on the sex offender registry. If David Marshall had been fully aware of William's situation, there is a possibility that he might not have shot William that morning in Corinth, Maine. It is obvious that placement on the registry can be dangerous to the registrants and the state must accept that responsibility knowing that the public has a right to know if a violent sexual predator is living or working in their community. It is important for the public to understand that not everyone on the sex offender registry is a threat to society – maybe some should not even be on the registry. We know how to improve the sex offender registry to make it more user friendly to the public and more efficient. Those changes need to be made as soon as possible.

Not Paranoia - Educated Awareness

One of the predominant findings contained in these chapters is the need to raise awareness levels of changes in children's behaviors or attitudes. Children who are sexually molested sometimes send messages trying to alert others about their nightmarish experiences. It may not be a direct plea from the child. Unfortunately, it usually is not that straight forward and easy to detect. Remember Marie, who as a young victim, wore her clothes inside out in an attempt to tell someone, anyone, that something was terribly wrong in her life? Children may ask for help in many ways when sexual assaults exist in their lives. This book leads us down the painful path to the realization of the importance of staying alert to subtle clues and changes in a child's personality that could be warnings of sexual abuse.

One of the reasons it's difficult to discover that sexual abuse of children is occurring is because sexual predators have such clever disguises. As we have learned, there is no limit to the creativity employed by pedophiles. Clergy, teachers, police officers, and the adoring family member, just to name a few, live and work among us every day. The lesson to be learned is - always be aware of your child and those children around you. Do not rely on the quintessential image of what a sexual predator would look like – most are not recognizable by appearance.

We know that when a proposed law has a child's name attached it should be viewed with caution and suspicion. The "name" usually means the law is motivated by a reaction to a heinous crime against a child and therefore the issue requires attention. The efforts are always well intended, but red flags need to be raised regarding these often ill-informed attempts to fix a problem quickly and always with media fanfare.

The Adam Walsh Act, although not done hastily, was named after the son of a well-known television personality, John Walsh. Chapter four tells the story and we learned that trying to craft sex offender legislation at the federal level to fit unique philosophies and traditions of each state is problematic – maybe impossible. State solutions versus reactive federal laws may make more sense. The success or failure of the questionable Adam Walsh Act will help answer that question. The "Plan," detailed in this book, provides guidance for adapting this federal law to make it more workable here.

One of the most important achievements of this book is shining the public light on the Maine Computer Crimes Unit and all other ICAC's (Internet Crimes Against Children) around the country. They rescue sexually abused children! What else rises to that level of importance? The CCU needs to be the highest priority for funding and overall support by the government and the public. Unfortunately, these ICAC's have to fight for basic funding from state budgets, notwithstanding the fact that they arguably perform the most important function in government. Once the public realizes the critical role played by the Computer Crimes Unit, lawmakers will follow suit – hopefully with the commitment and determination necessary to allow the Computer Crimes Units to reach their full potential in their efforts to rescue kids who are subjected to terrible abuse.

Improving the efficiency and organizational structure of the Computer Crimes Unit and passing new laws that provide more suitable punishment for the sex offenses committed against children are time sensitive. Many states, including Maine, have lenient sentencing laws for sex offenses committed against children compared to federal laws. It's time to bring Maine into line with federal sentencing standards.

Learning about sexual fetishes might seem humorous, even entertaining. But it's important to remember that these same fetishes, when focused toward children, are inappropriate and dangerous. Understanding the various fetishes and what motivates fetishists is part of the overall education needed by parents and those who supervise children. An innocent looking playground can be the fertile field for visual sexual attacks on unsuspecting children. Awareness of the potential for pedophilic behavior hidden among the inconspicuous observers is essential. Teaching children and adults about proper attire for children when playing outside is also very important and is one of those precautions that have been naively overlooked.

An In-Depth Discussion with Sex Offenders

Interviewing convicted sex offenders – looking them in the eye and listening as they describe their journeys leading up to and becoming fully involved in the world of sex offenders triggered every conceivable emotion. A child porn addict provides readers with a unique perspective on the slide into the destructive world of child pornography, a journey that underscored the critical ingredients necessary to the success of this deviant industry – the sexual assault of children and those who will pay to watch.

Learning the details of a husband and wife acting as a team as they sexually molest a 9-year old girl has highlighted yet another dimension in the realm of sexual predators. Christopher's description of his thought process leading up to the sexual assaults on his victim provides valuable insights into how one sex offender thinks, rationalizes and acts on his sexual desires. Still, imagining how the little girl had to struggle with her ordeal as a child and now as an adult is heartbreaking. The victims are always the losers and all of the rationalization in the world does not change that fact.

An Unbelievable Experience

Disgust – heartache – sadness – even hate. These were some of the emotions that dominated my mind and soul for 11 months while I researched and wrote this book. Witnessing the terrorized eyes of an innocent 3-year old toddler after being subjected to continued sexual assaults unleashed tormented images of suffering that refused to leave my mind…and without warning they reappear randomly in a confused and sad little face saying, "Remember me!"

Sleepless nights were all part of the experience usually caused by my brain spinning, sometimes out of control, searching for better ways to increase awareness of the dangers to children by pedophiles and sexual predators.

The bad news -- there will always be the *evil* who prey on the innocent.

The good news -- we have found a better way to protect the *innocent* - and it's contained in this book.

The End

THE EVIL AND THE INNOCENT

NOTES

Footnote Reference Number

1. Aull, Elbert. "Joseph Tellier, the sex offender shunned by Maine towns, dies." Portland Press Herald. 8 Sep. 2007

2. "Ex-coach charged with abusing boys." Portland Press Herald. 6 Nov. 2011: A3

3. Matthew Ruel. Maine Department of Public Safety.

5. John Doe v. District Attorney et al. Maine Supreme Judicial Court Decision 2007 ME 139 (25 Sep. 2007)

6. Maine. Autopsy Report: Joseph Gray, case # 06-00590_A. Augusta: Chief Medical Examiner. 10/1/06

7. Maine. Autopsy Report: William Elliott, case # 06-00591_A. Augusta: Chief Examiner. 10/1/06

8. "The Fifth Estate – Avenging Angel." Canadian Broadcasting Corporation 10/22/11

9. Clark, Amy S. "Sex Offender Murder Suspect Kills Self." CBS News. 17 Apr. 2006. 1/17/11

10. Hahn, Roger. "Biblical and Theological Resources for Growing Christians – 1 Corinthians." 10/23/11

11. Pate, David. "A Sex Offender'sStory." Canadian Broadcasting Corporation News. 25 Apr. 2006. 6/20/11

12. Russell, Eric. "Sex offender? No thanks, I'll take prison." Bangor Daily News. 15 Apr. 2011. 4/17/11

13. Wright, Richard G., ed. Sex Offender Laws – Failed Policies, New Directions. New York: Springer Publishing Co. 2009

14. "Real Time Acute Dynamic Sex Offender Risk Management." New York times.

15. Maxwell, Trevor. "Child Porn Convictions Cap Downfall of Prosecutor." Portland Press Herald. 24 Aug. 2011: A6

16. Burke, Jason, Amelia Gentleman, and Philip Willan. "British Link to 'Snuff' Videos." Guardian/The Observer. 1 Oct. 2000

17. Rhoda, Erin. "Teacher pleads guilty to making kid-porn photos." Morning Sentinel. 16 June 2011: C1

18. Williams, Christopher. "Hypnotist/Actor Convicted of Sex Assault on Minor." Lewiston Sun Journal. 26 Jan. 2011 1/26/11

19. Steves, Brittany and Rachel Friese. "The Documentary of the Case of Adam Walsh." 7/3/11

20. " 'America's Most Wanted' Statement on Reports of Possible Adam Walsh/Jeffrey Dahmer Connection." 6 Feb. 2007 http://www.amw.com/features/feature_story_detail.cfm?id=1421 7/3/11

21. Toole, Ottis. "Killer of 'Most Wanted' Host's Son Identified." 16 December 2008. 11 July 2011 http://en.wikipedia.org/wiki/Ottis_Tolle

22. Grinberg, Emanuella. "5 Years Later Struggle to Comply with Federal Sex Offender Law." CNN Justice 28 July 2011.

23. same as # 22

24. McPherson, Lori. "Update: Practitioner's Guide to the Adam Walsh Act." National Center for the Prosecution of Child Abuse vol 20: numbers 9-11.

25. Maine. State Police Computer Crimes Unit. Lang, Sergeant Glenn. Narrative.

26. Toole, Ottis. Interview with a Serial Killer. Dist. By Guilford Ghost. 1993.

27. United States. Federal Bureau of Investigation. Innocent Images National Initiative. "Child Pornography/Child Sexual Exploitation," 8 July 2011-11-18

28. Maine. State Police Computer Unit. "Tara Series." 11 Aug. 2011-11-18

29. United States. Federal Bureau of Investigation. "Violent Child Abuser and Child Pornography Producer Sentenced." 5 Mar. 2009. 8 July 2011.

30. State of Maine v. Tina Bickart. Maine Supreme Judicial Court. Decision 2009 ME 7 (20 January 2009).

31. State of Maine v. Benjamin S. Cook. Maine Supreme Judicial Court. Decision 2011 ME 94 (25 Aug. 2011).

34. Metropolitan Correctional Center. 10 Sep. 2011. http://en.wikipedia. org/Metropolitan_Correctional_Center,_New_York_City

35. "Penile Plethysmograph." The Skeptics Dictionary. 10 Oct. 2011. http://skepdic.com/penilep.html

36. State of Maine v. Thompson. Maine Supreme Judicial Court. Decision 1997 ME 109 (21 May 1997).

37. Maine. Maine Sex Offender Registry. Profile: Milton Allen Thompson.

38. Rhoda, Erin. "Ex-teacher Gets 16 Years for Porn." Morning Sentinel. 9 Nov. 2011: page C1

39. Dowd, Maureen. "Personal foul at Penn State." New York times. 9 Nov. 2011.

40. U.S. Department of Justice, University of New Hampshire, Survey, "Child Pornography Possessors Arrested in Internet-Related Crimes."

CPSIA information can be obtained at www.ICGtesting.com
Printed in the USA
BVOW032357040712

294311BV00001B/7/P